The WetFeet Insider Guide to Careers in Non-Profits and Government Agencies

2004 Edition

Helping you make smarter career decisions.

WetFeet Inc.

609 Mission Street
Suite 400
San Francisco, CA 94105

Phone: (415) 284-7900 or 1-800-926-4JOB
Fax: (415) 284-7910
E-mail: info@wetfeet.com
Website: www.wetfeet.com

The WetFeet Insider Guide to Careers in Non-Profits and Government Agencies

ISBN: 1-58207-315-5

Photocopying Is Prohibited

Table of Contents

The Industries at a Glance

Opportunity Overview

- Entry-level and midcareer jobs exist for people with degrees in just about any area of non-profit or government.

- Paid internships are common for government positions, but unlikely in the non-profit sector, where you'll be working for free.

- It's a crowded market—interest in working for non-profits or the government is booming. While non-profits aren't really increasing their hiring rates, a number of government agencies, especially in security and foreign affairs, are.

Major Pluses about Careers in Non-Profits/Government Agencies

- You'll really, really care about your job.

- You'll be able to make a difference relatively quickly on issues that matter to you.

- There's a lot of job security, especially in government positions.

Major Minuses about Careers in Non-Profits/Government Agencies

- The pay is substantially less than what you'd make in a similar position in the private sector.

- The amount of bureaucratic paperwork in government positions is enormous.

- The lack of structure in non-profits can be challenging—you're often doing a little bit of everything.

- Politics and policy affect your work, and if the administration or management changes to one you don't support, you'll have to think about moving on.

Recruiting Overview

- Non-profits generally don't recruit, while large federal agencies recruit for almost all positions—recruiting takes place on most major campuses and at career fairs, industry trade shows, and conferences.

- Both non-profit and government organizations have extensive job listings on their websites, so check those regularly.

- The hiring process at both types of organizations can be lengthy—non-profits often don't have the resources to quickly respond to resumes, and government employment moves at a typical bureaucratic pace.

- Internships or volunteering is one of the best ways to get your foot in the door.

The Industries

- Overview

- The Bottom Line

- Industry Trends

- Non-Profit and Government Lingo

- Industry Rankings

- Breakdown of Industries

Overview

Maybe you're a college student and you don't think you want a career in corporate America; maybe you're already working in business, and you KNOW you don't want a career in corporate America. There's nothing at all attractive to you about giving up 40 to 50 (or more) hours a week to work on projects or products you don't really care about. You'd rather use your skills to serve society than develop or sell a new enterprise software package without which the world would do just fine (or a new tax shelter for high-net-worth individuals, or a new super-absorbent bathroom tissue, or . . . you get the idea). To you, the trade-off of a lower salary and a smaller chance of getting rich are totally worth it, if you can do something real to help children learn or people eat or protect your country or the environment. (How many people really get rich working in business, anyway?)

Still with us? Then you're a good candidate for a career in non-profit or government. And, these days, you're not alone. Whether it's because of the demise of the dot coms, the spate of layoffs across the business landscape, or the terrorist attacks of September 11, 2001, many people seem to have changed their career focus from getting rich quick to doing something meaningful for themselves and for society. Both government and non-profit organizations are seeing a huge surge in applicants, which is good news for the country and the world, but which can be bad news for job seekers.

Non-Profits

Non-profit organizations are businesses designed to make change, and not in the monetary sense. Granted 501(c)3, or tax-exempt, status by the government, these organizations focus on a wide variety of causes, including everything

from the Africa Fund, which promotes human rights, education, and people-to-people exchanges with African countries, to the National Breast Cancer Foundation. Many non-profit interest groups are located in Washington, DC, where they lobby government on behalf of their causes; others have offices near state legislatures, where they lobby for the passage of legislation favorable to their causes.

Non-profits derive their operating revenue from foundations, government grants, membership dues, and fees for services they provide. They typically attract people who are passionate about solving social problems. The big upside of working in this sector is that you can make a positive impact on behalf of your organization's cause; the downside is that most jobs in the non-profit sector don't pay very well.

Non-profits and charitable organizations are becoming much more entrepreneurial, learning lessons from the private sector about how to operate more efficiently and do more with less by adopting marketing techniques to enhance their fund-raising efforts, or even starting their own small businesses to help generate income to fund social programs.

Government

Some 20 million people work for government—agencies and departments that on a federal, state, or local level handle issues as diverse as highway construction and the protection of wilderness areas, public health programs and subsidies to tobacco farmers, the space program, and fireworks displays on the Fourth of July. Governments collect taxes and use them to fund programs. That includes everything from a small-town government filling potholes on Main Street, to a big city providing police and firefighting services, to a state issuing drivers' licenses, to the federal government sending troops into combat or making Medicare payments to a long-term health care facility for the elderly poor.

Federal and state legislators make laws, and city and county supervisors pass ordinances. Executive agencies—from the White House to the state house to city hall—issue regulations. Governments employ armies of civil servants, bureaucrats, lawyers, and specialists of all kinds to implement their policies and staff their programs. These include people who analyze policy and draft legislation for U.S. senators, people who issue building permits at town hall, and everyone in between.

One way to think about the immense range of careers in government is to consider the broad categories the U.S. Office of Personnel Management uses to direct job seekers looking for careers that match their skills and abilities: Business Detail (think: accountants, security guards, etc.); Humanitarian (doctors, nurses, social workers, and chaplains); Leading-Influencing (policy analysts, law clerks, and Internal Revenue Service agents); Mechanical (air-conditioner repairmen, aerospace engineers, and boat designers); Plants and Animals (agricultural inspectors, zookeepers, cemetery caretakers, and park rangers); Protective (border patrol agents, Securities and Exchange Commission regulators, federal corrections officers, and gaming regulators); Scientific (cartographers, horticulturalists, and infectious disease researchers); and, of course, Other (everything from museum curators and interior designers to barbers and fork-lift operators).

It's important to note that while the federal government is gigantic—it employed nearly 2.9 million people in 2000—there are far more jobs available across the country at the state and local government level; in 2000, close to 18 million people were employed by state and local governments.

Even though most employees in this sector enjoy excellent benefits, there can be downsides to working in government. For one thing, the pay is often lower in government positions than in their private-sector equivalents. And in many government positions, jobs are politicized: Your priorities (and the culture of your workplace) can change with the election cycle, and the program you're working on or the representative you work for may not even be around next year.

Working for an International Organization

Many non-profits and government agencies have international opportunities—Habitat for Humanity and the Red Cross, for example, work across borders, and the U.S. State Department is primarily concerned with overseas policy. If you don't have dual nationality or a valid work permit for another country, it will be very hard to become a direct employee of an international agency registered in another country. The most obvious organization for U.S. citizens is the United Nations—this is also difficult to get into. (See "Key Government Agencies" in "The Organizations" chapter.)

The Bottom Line

It can be hard getting a job in non-profit or government. The hiring process is often lengthy, and the competition can be fierce. For example, one foundation executive director in California recently received 400 applications for a program manager position. Persistence pays off, though. If you're committed to a particular issue, don't hide it. Volunteering and interning are two very good ways to get in the door at a non-profit. If you want a government internship, however, you'll most likely have to be a student. That said, a number of government agencies are increasing their hiring numbers, especially in the areas of security and foreign affairs, whereas non-profits for the most part aren't. So you may find it less of an uphill battle to land a paying government job than even a non-paying internship at a non-profit.

Industry Trends

Homeland Security

September 11, 2001, made clear the threat of terrorism to the United States. In response, the federal government gathered together a bunch of previously separate government entities, including the Coast Guard, the Border Patrol, Customs, and the Immigration and Naturalization Service, to centralize their efforts to protect the United States, avoid redundancy, and to allow different organizations to cross purposes. President Bush has made Homeland Security a priority for his administration, resulting in strong budgets in this sector. This means more career opportunities for you, the job seeker, if you're interested in intelligence gathering, analysis, or working for the Border Patrol, Customs, or other entities under the Homeland Security umbrella.

Meanwhile, over in the non-profit arena, some are complaining that Homeland Security is eroding citizens' civil rights and stifling the dissenting voice of non-profits that advocate policies opposed federal government practices like IRS audits of liberal non-profits and attempts to limit or eliminate federal funds for certain non-profits.

Government Outsourcing

In recent years, "reinventing government" has been a catchphrase among policymakers. On the ground, this means that governments are increasingly outsourcing functions and services that were traditionally handled by government agencies to the private sector. For example, municipal governments traditionally provided garbage-removal services in many cities; these days, however, private

trash companies often provide these services. The thinking is that the profit motive drives private enterprises to be more efficient than government entities, thus driving down the total cost of outsourced services to society. The reality is less clear, however. The cost of services to society can remain the same (or even increase) even when private enterprises are more efficient than the government service providers they replace, since private enterprises need to charge more for their services than they actually cost to make a profit.

And there are other, less obvious costs. For example, it's more difficult for governments to oversee the operations of contract service providers than those of government agencies; indeed, there have been many examples of abuse by contract government service providers. And many workers employed by contract service providers receive lower pay and weaker benefits than did the government workers they replaced. And among those remaining in government employ, workplace morale can become a factor in areas more likely to be outsourced.

The Bad Economy

After the boom-boom years of the 1990s, corporate earnings growth is down, stock values are down, and layoffs are way, way up. This means less money is available for governments, thanks to the shrinking tax base, and for non-profits, which often depend on the largesse of corporations, individuals, and governments to fund their operations. Indeed, the federal government and many state and local governments are now facing budget crises—they don't have the income to fund all of the programs and projects they'd like to move forward. And non-profits are facing lean times in terms of fund raising. None of this is good news for job seekers.

Measuring the Metrics

In an effort to increase their efficiency and effectiveness, governments and non-profits are increasingly adopting management techniques from business. For example, they're increasingly relying on metrics—quantitative measurements—to gauge their success in achieving goals. This means that government and non-profit programs, as well as the staffers who drive them, are increasingly being evaluated by their ability to meet the metrical goals set for them by management (in tandem with funders, in the case of non-profits). This can be a good thing or a bad thing, depending on whether the right metrics are being used to measure success. It's a lot easier to measure a business's success—just look at the bottom line—and how individuals in that business are contributing to that bottom line than it is to measure non-profit or government success, where the goal is not to make a profit but to achieve a mission that is difficult to quantify.

For example, how do you measure whether you're doing the best job possible to serve disabled students if you're working at a non-profit serving that population? There are metrics to measure whether you're succeeding in your mission, but they can be much more difficult to identify than the financial measurements businesses use to measure their progress and success.

Non-Profit and Government Lingo

At-risk. Used by non-profits to describe socially or economically disadvantaged people: people who are poor, uneducated, unemployed, disabled, and/or from a minority population, who are "at risk" of falling through the cracks of society.

Challenge grant. A charitable contribution made on the condition that the funded organization will raise additional funds elsewhere; meant to spur other potential donors to give.

Charitable remainder trust. A donation to charity that allows the donor to continue to use and/or earn income from the donated money or property while he or she remains alive.

Clients. The people a non-profit aims to serve. The term is meant to lend dignity to the act of receiving charity.

Community foundation. Community foundations raise funds from a variety of donors in a community or region, and generally make grants to non-profit charities in the community or region.

Constituents. The specific citizens an elected official represents—e.g., the people living in a U.S. Representative's district. Government version of "clients."

Corporate foundation. Corporate foundations are established as separate entities by corporations to make charitable grants.

Endowment. Donation to establish and run a program or facility (e.g., a scholarship or an arts series); the endowment donation is invested and the income on the investment or investments is used to run the program or facility on an ongoing basis.

Foggy Bottom. The U.S. Department of State.

Independent foundation. Independent foundations usually consist of an endowment made by a single individual or family, and use the income from the endowment to make philanthropic grants.

In-kind gift. Donation of equipment or supplies rather than money.

KSAs. Knowledge, skills, and abilities. You need to prove via an essay that you have KSAs that match the requirements of the job you're interested in if you're applying for most federal positions.

Mission statement. The cornerstone of any non-profit, this summarizes the purpose of the organization. Can serve as a useful management tool for keeping employees on the same page.

Operating foundation. Operating foundations focus on funding their own non-profit programs.

P.A.C. Political action committee. Organizations created to raise money to elect or defeat political candidates. Usually exist to advance the cause of businesses, labor organizations, and/or social or political ideologies.

Public trust designation. Categorization for federal jobs that require a background check as part of the hiring process.

Schedule C employees. Federal government employees who've been appointed to their positions at the discretion of the President.

Stakeholders. All those who have an emotional and/or financial investment in a non-profit—e.g., a non-profit's clients, staff, board members, and funders, and the surrounding community.

Term appointment. Non-permanent government job filled by appointment. Lasts one to four years. Appointee receives the same benefits as permanent government employees.

Veterans' preference. Refers to the fact that U.S. military veterans receive extra consideration when they apply for competitive civil service positions. An advantage in the application process, but in no way a guarantee of landing the job.

Industry Rankings

Rank	Name	2001 Operating Income ($M)
	Top 100 Non-Profits by 2001 Income	
1	Lutheran Services in America	7,655.0
2	The National Council of YMCAs	4,123.1
3	American Red Cross	2,711.6
4	Catholic Charities USA	2,621.2
5	United Jewish Communities	2,230.6
6	Goodwill Industries International	1,940.9
7	Salvation Army	1,914.9
8	Fidelity Investments Charitable Gift Fund	1,250.6
9	Boys & Girls Club of America	997.8
10	American Cancer Society, Inc.	922.9
11	The Metropolitan Museum of Art	762.8
12	The Nature Conservancy	731.9
13	Boy Scouts of America	726.8
14	Habitat for Humanity International	689.7
15	Gifts In Kind International	681.1
16	Girl Scouts of the USA	680.0
17	Planned Parenthood Federation of America	661.3
18	America's Second Harvest	652.2
19	YWCA of the USA	646.0
20	Volunteers of America	591.7
21	Easter Seals 5	583.4
22	Public Broadcasting Service	536.5
23	World Vision	528.6

Top 100 Non-Profits by 2001 Income (cont'd)

Rank	Name	2001 Operating Income ($M)
24	American Heart Association	502.7
25	Smithsonian Institution	499.1
26	United Cerebral Palsy Associations	483.2
27	AmeriCares Foundation	464.9
28	Feed the Children	457.6
29	CARE USA	423.3
30	City of Hope	382.7
31	Campus Crusade for Christ, Inc.	373.3
32	ALSAC-St. Jude's Children's Research Hospital	352.1
33	Dana Farber Cancer Institute	328.9
34	Food For The Poor	320.8
35	Catholic Relief Services	320.1
36	Wildlife Conservation Society	311.7
37	Metropolitan Opera Assoc., Inc.	289.8
38	Shriners Hospitals for Children	266.9
39	Fred Hutchinson Cancer Research Center	256.7
40	March of Dimes	217.9
41	Special Olympics International, Inc.	206.6
42	Big Brothers/Big Sisters of America	204.9
43	Colonial Williamsburg Foundation	200.2
44	US Fund for UNICEF	199.2
45	WGBH Educational Foundation	192.7
46	American Museum of Natural History	185.1
47	United Negro College Fund, Inc.	178.9
48	Trinity Broadcasting Network	177.8
49	Ducks Unlimited Inc.	176.4

Top 100 Non-Profits by 2001 Income (cont'd)

Rank	Name	2001 Operating Income ($M)
50	Girls Incorporated	176.0
51	The Christian Broadcasting Network	175.4
52	Save the Children Federation, Inc.	173.3
53	Institute of International Education	171.4
54	American Lung Association	167.3
55	American Diabetes Association	166.7
56	Art Institute of Chicago	164.6
57	Vanguard Charitable Endowment Program	164.2
58	Alzheimer's Disease & Related Disorders Assoc.	162.9
59	Museum Of Modern Art	162.6
60	Girls and Boys Town	158.2
61	National Multiple Sclerosis Society	156.3
62	International Rescue Committee	156.1
63	The Christian and Missionary Alliance	154.9
64	The Leukemia & Lymphoma Society	153.4
65	Young Life	153.2
66	Muscular Dystrophy Assoc.	152.4
67	Educational Broadcasting Corp.	151.1
68	Samaritan's Purse	150.6
69	Juvenile Diabetes Foundation International	148.6
70	Map International, Inc.	146.4
71	Citizens' Scholarship Foundation of America	143.8
72	J.F. Kennedy Center for the Performing Arts	143.4
73	National Assoc. for the Exchange of Ind. Resources	141.2
74	National Mental Health Association	140.7
75	Children's Television Workshop/Sesame Workshop	137.7

Top 100 Non-Profits by 2001 Income (cont'd)

Rank	Name	2001 Operating Income ($M)
76	Christian Aid Ministries	133.8
77	Arthritis Foundation	132.7
78	Schwab Fund For Charitable Giving	131.6
79	Make A Wish Foundation	130.4
80	Cystic Fibrosis Foundation	129.7
81	Rotary Foundation of Rotary International	129.5
82	Christian Children's Fund	126.9
83	Trust For Public Land	126.3
84	National Gallery of Art	123.9
85	Junior Achievement, Inc.	121.5
86	Focus on the Family	121.3
87	SIL International (Summer Inst of Linguistics, Inc.)	121.3
88	Disabled American Veterans	120.0
89	World Wildlife Fund	118.1
90	Covenant House	117.9
91	Museum of Fine Arts, Boston	117.6
92	Compassion International	109.8
93	Wycliffe Bible Translators	108.9
94	National Wildlife Federation & Endowment	105.6
95	Jewish Board of Family and Children's Services	104.0
96	Project HOPE	102.3
97	National Jewish Medical and Research Center	99.7
98	The Carter Center	97.7
99	NY Police & Fire Widows' & Children's Benefit	97.6
100	Local Initiatives Support Corporation	96.8

Source: *The NonProfit Times.*

Top 50 U.S. Foundations by Asset Size

Rank	Name (State)	Assets ($M)	As of Fiscal Year-End
1	Bill & Melinda Gates Foundation (WA)	32,751.5	12/31/01
2	Lilly Endowment Inc. (IN)	12,814.4	12/31/01
3	The Ford Foundation (NY)	9,300.1	9/30/02
4	J. Paul Getty Trust (CA)	8,793.5	6/30/01
5	The Robert Wood Johnson Foundation (NJ)	8,012.4	12/31/02
6	The David and Lucile Packard Foundation (CA)	6,196.5	12/31/01
7	The William and Flora Hewlett Foundation (CA)	6,080.7	12/31/01
8	W. K. Kellogg Foundation (MI)	5,530.5	8/31/02
9	The Starr Foundation (NY)	4,781.0	12/31/01
10	John D. and Catherine T. MacArthur Foundation (IL)	4,215.9	12/31/01
11	The Andrew W. Mellon Foundation (NY)	4,135.6	12/31/01
12	The Pew Charitable Trusts (PA)	3,753.6	12/31/02
13	The California Endowment (CA)	3,366.3	2/28/02
14	The Rockefeller Foundation (NY)	2,679.1	12/31/02
15	The Annie E. Casey Foundation (MD)	2,592.4	12/31/01
16	Charles Stewart Mott Foundation (MI)	2,460.2	12/31/01
17	Robert W. Woodruff Foundation, Inc. (GA)	2,422.6	12/31/01
18	The Kresge Foundation (MI)	2,416.0	12/31/01
19	The Annenberg Foundation (PA)	2,354.8	6/30/02
20	Casey Family Programs (WA)	2,349.8	12/31/01
21	The Duke Endowment (NC)	2,084.8	12/31/02
22	The Harry and Jeanette Weinberg Foundation, Inc. (MD)	1,936.3	2/28/02
23	The McKnight Foundation (MN)	1,877.7	12/31/01
24	Robert R. McCormick Tribune Foundation (IL)	1,855.0	12/31/02
25	The New York Community Trust (NY)	1,785.2	12/31/01
26	John S. and James L. Knight Foundation (FL)	1,718.2	12/31/02

Top 50 U.S. Foundations by Asset Size (cont'd)

Rank	Name (State)	Assets ($M)	As of Fiscal Year-End
27	Ewing Marion Kauffman Foundation (MO)	1,687.5	6/30/02
28	Carnegie Corporation of New York (NY)	1,627.7	9/30/02
29	The Freeman Foundation (NY)	1,619.1	12/31/01
30	Donald W. Reynolds Foundation (NV)	1,524.2	12/31/01
31	Doris Duke Charitable Foundation (NY)	1,444.8	12/31/01
32	Richard King Mellon Foundation (PA)	1,393.6	12/31/02
33	The James Irvine Foundation (CA)	1,378.4	12/31/01
34	Houston Endowment, Inc. (TX)	1,367.7	12/31/01
35	The Cleveland Foundation (OH)	1,312.2	12/31/02
36	The Wallace Foundation (NY)	1,303.3	12/31/01
37	W. M. Keck Foundation (CA)	1,263.9	12/31/01
38	The Brown Foundation, Inc. (TX)	1,183.6	6/30/02
39	Alfred P. Sloan Foundation (NY)	1,171.0	12/31/02
40	Marin Community Foundation (CA)	1,150.6	6/30/01
41	The Chicago Community Trust and Affiliates (IL)	1,018.3	9/30/02
42	Lumina Foundation for Education, Inc. (IN)	991.3	12/31/01
43	Walton Family Foundation, Inc. (AR)	948.7	12/31/01
44	Kimbell Art Foundation (TX)	933.1	12/31/01
45	The Moody Foundation (TX)	926.9	12/31/01
46	Howard Heinz Endowment (PA)	907.7	12/31/01
47	The Henry Luce Foundation, Inc. (NY)	905.3	12/31/01
48	The William Penn Foundation (PA)	904.5	12/31/02
49	The Joyce Foundation (IL)	868.3	12/31/01
50	Horace W. Goldsmith Foundation (NY)	864.6	12/31/01

Source: The Foundation Center.

2002 Federal Outlays by Agency

Department	Est. 2002 Budget Outlay ($B)
Legislative Branch	3.6
Judicial Branch	5.0
Agriculture	76.6
Commerce	5.5
Defense-Military	330.6
Education	47.6
Energy	19.1
Health and Human Services	459.4
Housing and Urban Development	30.9
Interior	10.3
Justice	23.1
Labor	58.6
State	11.1
Transportation	60.8
Treasury	382.6
Veterans Affairs	51.5
Corps of Engineers	5.0
Other Defense–Civil Programs	35.5
Environmental Protection Agency	7.8
Executive Office of the President	0.5
Federal Emergency Management Administration	5.8
General Services Administration	0.6
International Assistance Programs	13.3
National Aeronautics and Space Administration	14.5
National Science Foundation	4.6
Office of Personnel Management	54.3
Social Security Administration (on-budget)	46.9
Social Security Administration (off-budget)	445.7

Source: Statistical Abstract of the United States, 2002.

Federal Civilian Employment by Branch or Agency

Branch/Agency	Employees, 2001	% Change, 1995–2001
Legislative Branch	2,709,956	−7
Judicial Branch	33,810	17
Executive Branch		
State	28,122	13
Treasury	148,186	−5
Defense	671,591	−19
Justice	127,783	24
Interior	75,846	−1
Agriculture	108,540	−4
Commerce	40,289	10
Labor	16,376	1
Health & Human Services	64,343	8
Housing & Urban Development	10,178	−14
Transportation	65,542	3
Energy	16,054	−18
Education	4,683	−6
Veterans Affairs	225,893	−14
Independent Agencies		
Federal Reserve	1,680	−1
Commodities Futures Trading Commission	551	1
Consumer Product Safety Commission	479	−1
Environmental Protection Agency	18,095	1
EEO Commission	2,910	4
FCC	2,004	−5
FDIC	6,402	−57
FEMA	6,147	17

Federal Civilian Employment by Branch or Agency (cont'd)

Branch/Agency	Employees, 2001	% Change, 1995–2001
Independent Agencies (cont'd)		
Federal Trade Commission	1,052	6
General Services Administration	14,016	−15
NASA	18,918	−13
National Archives & Records	2,878	2
National Labor Relations Board	2,110	3
Nuclear Regulatory Commission	2,871	−11
Office of Personnel Management	3,349	−23
Peace Corps	1,019	−14
SEC	3,049	7
Small Business Administration	4,219	−17
Smithsonian Institution	4,981	−9
Social Security Administration	65,351	−2
Tennessee Valley Authority	13,430	−19
U.S. Information Agency	2,372	−68
U.S. Postal Service	847,821	0

Source: Statistical Abstract of the United States, 2002.

Federal Agencies Employing 500 or More Full-Time Officers with Authority to Carry Firearms and Make Arrests	
Agency	**Officers, 2000**
INS	17,654
Federal Bureau of Prisons	13,557
FBI	11,523
Customs	10,522
DEA	4,161
Secret Service	4,039
Administrative Office of the U.S. Courts	3,599
U.S. Postal Inspection Service	3,412
U.S. Marshals Service	2,735
IRS	2,726
National Park Service	2,188
ATF	1,967
U.S. Capitol Police	1,199
U.S. Forest Service	888
U.S. Fish and Wildlife Service	586
Source: Statistical Abstract of the United States, 2002.	

Breakdown of Industries

Non-Profits

More than 25 types of non-profit organizations are recognized by the IRS, from the sacred (religious groups) to the obscure (black lung trusts). There are a number of ways to break down the non-profit sector. For instance, non-profits can be divided into those that focus on lobbying government on behalf of a cause (interest groups such as the National Rifle Association) and those that focus on providing services to society (such as museums or homes for pregnant teens).

To get a sense of the variety of non-profits, here's a short list of causes and the organizations that serve them:

Cause	Organizations
Arts and education	Friends of the Library
	Washington Ballet
	New York Philharmonic
	Boy Scouts, Girl Scouts
	4H
	National Center on Family Literacy
Civil and human rights	Amnesty International
	American Civil Liberties Union
	National Immigration Forum
	NAACP
	Planned Parenthood
The environment	Environmental Defense Fund
	National Wildlife Federation
	Nature Conservancy
	Sierra Club
Economic and social justice	American Association of Retired Persons
	Center for the Child Care Workforce
	National Low Income Housing Coalition
	Salvation Army
	United Way

Alongside the large national and international non-profits are myriad locally based, smaller non-profits; like their bigger cousins, these break down by mission and include everything from community theater troupes to women's shelters to convalescent homes.

In addition, the non-profit arena includes non-profit charitable/philanthropic funds and foundations. These organizations have an endowment and/or solicit donations, which they use to fund grants to non-profit organizations. There are several types of foundations. Community foundations raise funds from a variety of donors in community or region; the Marin Community Foundation in California is one example. Corporate foundations are established as separate entities by corporations to make charitable grants. Independent foundations usually consist of an endowment made by a single individual or family; the Annie E. Casey Foundation is an example. Operating foundations focus on funding their own non-profit programs.

Government

The executive branch agencies comprise the largest group of federal government jobs, including the Social Security Administration, the Environmental Protection Agency, the Federal Bureau of Investigations, the National Endowment for the Humanities, the Bureau of Indian Affairs, and the Bureau of Engraving and Printing. There are also jobs available in agencies under the aegis of the judicial and legislative branches, such as in the Library of Congress or the Congressional Budget Office. There are two basic types of positions in the various government agencies: civil service positions and political appointments (also called Schedule C appointments).

Not all people with federal agency jobs are based in Washington, DC. Think of all those postal employees out on the streets of America, braving rain, sleet, and snow. Or the diplomat at the U.S. embassy in Cairo. Or the park ranger in Yellowstone National Park. Think of the bureaucrats in federal office buildings in every major U.S. city, the Bureau of Indian Affairs agent on some isolated reservation in New Mexico, the civilian technician maintaining communications gear in the tropical heat of Guam, the medical researcher culturing bacteria at the Centers for Disease Control in Atlanta.

Congressional jobs, on the other hand, are more concentrated geographically. Congress—the legislative branch—is divided into the House, which consists of one representative from each of 435 districts in the country (and several nonvoting delegates), and the Senate, which is made up of 100 senators, two from each state. Most people who work for the legislative branch of the federal government are based in Washington, DC. They are on the staffs of legislators or legislative agencies, such as the aforementioned Library of Congress. Representatives and senators also maintain staffs in their home districts and states. Every senator and representative hires a staff to assist with his or her job, and this is where many opportunities exist in Washington for young people, provided they have good educations and, usually, good connections.

Like the federal government, state governments consist of various executive-branch agencies along with a legislative body, all of which offer opportunities to job seekers. Similarly, local governments, including those of townships, counties, and cities, offer a range of political and agency job opportunities; consider public health, community development, and court administration.

The Organizations

- Key Non-Profits

- Key Government Agencies

Key Non-Profits

Following are profiles of some organizations that ranked high on the list of key non-profits.

American Cancer Society

Size: 2 million volunteers; 2001 revenue of $993 million
HQ location: Atlanta, GA
www.cancer.org

Founded in 1913, the American Cancer Society focuses on conducting cancer research, serving cancer patients and their families, preventing cancer through the education of the public, advocacy to influence public policy, and the education of health care providers. The organization has more than 3,400 local units across the country. It received its biggest boost in the 1930s, with the creation of the Women's Field Army, which took to the streets in khaki uniforms to raise money and educate the public about cancer, about which many had previously considered it impolite to talk.

In terms of successes, we'll let the American Cancer Society strut its own stuff: "Over the years, scientists supported by the American Cancer Society have established the link between cancer and smoking, demonstrated the effectiveness of the Pap smear, developed cancer fighting drugs and biological response modifiers such as interferon, dramatically increased the cure rate for childhood leukemia, proved the safety and effectiveness of mammography, and much, much more. All told, the Society has committed nearly $2.2 billion to research, funding 30 Nobel Prize winners, often early in their careers before they had received recognition and monetary support for their work."

The Organizations

American Red Cross

Size: 34,356 employees worldwide; 2002 revenue of $4.1 billion

HQ location: Falls Church, VA

Phone: 703-206-6000

www.redcross.org

The Red Cross is famous worldwide for providing disaster relief, health services, and education; it deals with about 67,000 cases each year in the United States. The American Red Cross gives aid to disaster victims and members of the U.S. military. It also runs blood drives and solicits tissue donations. Though it does work closely with the government in times of crisis, this is not a political organization. It's about helping people in dire straits, wherever and whoever they are. In fact, the Red Cross includes among its fundamental principles neutrality, impartiality, and independence. The Red Cross was created in 1863 in Switzerland; in 1881, Clara Barton was the first person to establish a lasting Red Cross Society in America. The Red Cross was deeply involved in 9/11 relief efforts—nearly 55,000 Red Cross workers mobilized in response.

America's Second Harvest

Size: 2002 revenue of $488 million

HQ location: Chicago, IL

Phone: 800-771-2303

www.americassecondharvest.org

America's Second Harvest in the nation's largest hunger-relief organization, overseeing 200 food banks and food-rescue programs. It serves 23 million hungry Americans annually, including eight million children. Key programs offered by America's Second Harvest include Community Kitchens, in which underemployed individuals make meals for hungry Americans while being

trained in food preparation skills; Disaster Relief, in which the organization provides relief supplies to emergency feeding centers serving disaster victims; the Fresh Food Initiative, which distributes fresh foods to hungry people; Kids Café, a meal service and nutrition education program for needy kids; the Seafood Initiative, which distributes donated fish to hungry Americans; Pallet for the Hungry, a program which gets growers and shippers working together to distribute fresh produce to the needy; the Production Alliance, through which companies use their philanthropy budgets and available production capacity to produce products for America's Second Harvest food banks and food-rescue programs; and Relief Fleet, which brings donated transportation together with donated food to feed hungry Americans.

Goodwill Industries International, Inc.

Size: 2002 revenue of $2.06 billion
HQ location: Bethesda, MD
Phone: 240-333-5200
www.goodwill.org

Goodwill serves people with workplace disadvantages and disabilities by providing them with job training and employment services. It's organized as a network of more than 200 local Goodwill organizations around the world. The organization raises funds via nearly 2,000 Goodwill thrift shops and by providing contract labor to businesses and government organizations. Goodwill has locations in Canada and 22 other countries outside the United States. Nearly 85 percent of Goodwill's revenue goes to job training, placement programs, and other community services. In 2002, Goodwill served 583,351 clients.

Habitat for Humanity International

Size: 1,700 affiliates nationwide, 70 international; 2002 revenue of $162 million

HQ location: Americus, GA

Phone: 229-924-6935

www.habitat.org

Since 1976, Habitat for Humanity has built more than 150,000 houses worldwide. Houses are sold to local buyers at no profit with no-interest mortgages. Habitat for Humanity has provided more than 750,000 people in more than 3,000 communities with safe, decent, affordable shelter. The organization depends on a loyal group of employees and volunteers, who pay their own way to help construct new buildings. Local affiliate non-profits conduct the on-the-ground work of Habitat for Humanity, taking applications from and choosing needy families to benefit from Habitat's services. Habitat for Humanity counts more than 2,100 active affiliates in 87 countries, including all 50 states of the United States, the District of Columbia, Guam, and Puerto Rico. Houses built by Habitat for Humanity cost as little as $800 in some developing countries to an average of $46,600 in the United States. Former President Jimmy Carter has been famously associated with Habitat for Humanity since 1984, lending his face and name to fund-raising efforts and spending time building houses. Habitat for Humanity is an ecumenical Christian non-profit.

The Nature Conservancy

Size: 3,000 employees worldwide; 2002 revenue of $923 million

HQ location: Arlington, VA

Phone: 800-628-6860

www.nature.org

Founded in 1951, the Nature Conservancy protects more than 116 million acres worldwide, the vast majority of them outside the United States, in about 1,400 preserves. Its mission is to "preserve the plants, animals, and natural communities that represent the diversity of life on Earth by protecting the lands and waters they need to survive." The Nature Conservancy's Campaign for Conservation, the largest private conservation campaign ever, is investing $1.25 billion to "save 200 of the world's Last Great Places." The Nature Conservancy's five major current initiatives are restoring fire-altered ecosystems, working to reduce the likelihood of significant climate change, protecting freshwater ecosystems, controlling the threat to biodiversity posed by non-native plant and animal species, and protecting oceans and coastal areas.

Planned Parenthood Federation of America

Size: 128 affiliates nationwide (300 employees in the national office); 2002 revenue of $693 million

HQ location: New York, NY

Phone: 212-541-7800

www.plannedparenthood.org

The nation's first birth control clinic was founded in 1916 by visionary Margaret Sanger. Both its supporters and critics are extremely vocal—it's seen as both a safe haven for women across the country as well as an aggressively pro-choice institution. Currently, Planned Parenthood is advocating against the Bush

administration's gag rule prohibiting federal funding of organizations that provide abortions. The organization also seems to make it into the newspapers far too frequently due to attacks on offices and staffers by pro-life (or, as Planned Parenthood puts it, "anti-choice") advocates. The organization has lots of opportunities for doctors, nurses, nurse practitioners, counselors, and so on, but it also employs folks in marketing, fund-raising, administration, and other typical business and non-profit functions.

Public Broadcasting Service

Size: 2003 operating revenue estimated at $322 million
HQ location: New York, NY
www.pbs.org

Created by Congress as an independent non-profit in 1967, the Public Broadcasting Service provides quality television programming to public television stations across the country. The organization does not produce TV programs, but rather acquires and distributes them to nearly 350 public stations. If you value television programs like Ken Burns' *Jazz*, *Frontline*, *NOVA*, *Masterpiece Theater*, or *The NewsHour* with Jim Lehrer, this might be the place for you. But TV is not all the organization focuses on. Departments within the organization include program acquisition, distribution, and promotion; education services; new media ventures; fund-raising support; engineering and technology development; and video marketing. PBS's Adult Learning Service offers multimedia educational courses. And PBS.org has Web pages for about 1,000 PBS television programs and specials, as well as other informative and educational content.

The Salvation Army

Size: 40,000 employees nationwide; 2001 net assets/liabilities of $2.3 billion

HQ location: Alexandria, VA

Phone: 703-684-5500

www.salvationarmy.org

Commonly associated with thrift stores and holiday bell-ringers, The Salvation Army, which was created by William Booth in England in 1865, is a global organization that fights its war against poverty with an impressive array of "generals," "soldiers," and other enlistees. In 2001, it assisted almost 40 million people with disaster relief, job placement services, food, shelter, and other services. Currently, it's working hard to serve the needy in Iraq. In the United States, The Salvation Army describes itself as a Christian evangelical organization. Indeed, its website includes the following copy: "Those who have drifted away from God and those estranged from their own religious affiliations are often attracted to The Salvation Army. They are first urged to seek Christ for pardon and deliverance from sin. Then they are encouraged to return to active memberships in their own churches or to enroll as soldiers in a corps community center."

Teach for America

Size: 150 employees, 1,700 teachers; 2001 net assets/liabilities of $22 million

HQ location: New York, NY

Phone: 800-832-1230

www.teachforamerica.org

Teach for America is the national corps of outstanding recent college graduates, of all academic majors, who commit two years to teach in public schools in low-income communities. Since its founding, the organization has placed more than 7,000 recent college graduates as teachers in some of the

nation's most under-resourced urban and rural schools. The organization was started by Wendy Kopp, who, as a senior at Princeton University in 1989, dreamed up the idea. Kopp developed a plan for the idea in her undergraduate senior thesis and then secured a seed grant from Mobil Corporation to get started. Corporations providing funding to Teach for America include American Express, AT&T, BellSouth, and Goldman Sachs.

United Way of America

Size: 1,400 affiliates nationwide; 2002 revenue of $5 billion

HQ location: Alexandria, VA

Phone: 703-836-7112

www.unitedway.org

United Way's approximately 1,400 affiliates are independently operated and run by local volunteers who help the organization achieve its mission: improving people's lives by mobilizing the power of their local communities. United Way operates by funding other non-profits—for example, Big Brothers/Big Sisters, the American Cancer Society, and the Boy and Girl Scouts. The organization offers career opportunities in Alexandria and across the country. United Way works closely with corporations, the U.S. government, and labor organizations (its relationship with the National Football League has probably contributed most to making the organization a household name).

Key Foundations

Bill & Melinda Gates Foundation

Size: 200 employees; 2002 assets of $24 billion
HQ location: Seattle, WA
Phone: 206-709-3140
www.gatesfoundation.org

While it's the largest foundation in the world, the Gates Foundation employs only 200 people full time—something it's been criticized for (it currently depends on outside evaluators to monitor the grants it gives out). But its intentions are good: In 2002, it anticipated making grants totaling almost $6 billion, with the majority spent in the areas of education and global health. Additionally, the Gates Foundation focuses on bringing libraries into the digital age and on programs in the Pacific Northwest. The Foundation was created in 2000.

David & Lucille Packard Foundation

Size: 160 employees; 2002 assets of $4.8 billion
HQ location: Los Altos, CA
Phone: 650-948-7658
www.packard.org

The Packard Foundation makes grants to programs in the following areas: conservation and science; population; and children, families, and communities. In addition to funding non-profits nationally and internationally, the Foundation has a focus on the Northern California Counties of San Mateo, Santa Clara, Santa Cruz, and Monterey. The Foundation made $230 million in grants in 2002 and has plans to make around $200 million in grants in 2003. The Foundation was founded in 1964 by David Packard, co-founder of the Hewlett-Packard Company, and his wife. At press time, the Foundation was looking for a president and CEO.

John D. and Catherine T. MacArthur Foundation

Size: 192 employees; 2002 assets of $4.2 billion

HQ location: Chicago, IL

Phone: 312-726-8000

www.macarthur.org

Created in 1978, the foundation bears the names of its founders, John D. MacArthur, who owned Bankers Life and Casualty Co., among other businesses, and Catherine T. MacArthur, who served as the foundation director for a time. The foundation supports efforts that include making communities healthy by ensuring that all of its members have their physical and mental heath and have equal access to opportunities; promoting international peace, ecosystems conservation, and responsible reproductive choices around the world; and supporting public-interest media projects and other special interest projects.

Finally, the MacArthur Fellows Program, one of the most prestigious fellowships around, provides unrestricted five-year stipends ranging from $30,000 to $75,000 to "exceptionally creative individuals, regardless of field of endeavor." Some famous MacArthur fellows of the past include Joseph Brodsky, John Ashbery, Henry Louis Gates, Jr., Cormac McCarthy, Errol Morris, Thomas Pynchon, Max Roach, Cindy Sherman, Susan Sontag, David Foster Wallace, Harold Bloom, Paul Ehrlich, and Stephen J. Gould.

Key Government Agencies

United States Agency for International Development (USAID)

Size: 2004 budget request of $9.6 billion
HQ location: Washington, DC
Phone: 202-712-4810
www.usaid.gov

This independent agency provides humanitarian and economic aid to countries around the world. Current important missions include development work in Afghanistan and addressing the food crisis in southern Africa. USAID focuses on agriculture, democracy and governance, economic growth and trade, the environment, education, and health. The organization was formed in 1961, when Congress mandated the separation of economic aid from military aid. Among its other projects, USAID is currently involved in rebuilding Iraq's power and education systems, giving food assistance to Iraq, supporting Afghan women, and supporting Kabul's first public radio station.

Central Intelligence Agency (CIA)

Size: undisclosed (est. number of employees in 2000 was 20,000)
HQ location: MacLean, VA
Phone: 703-482-0623
www.cia.gov

This most clandestine arm of the U.S. government is not actually all that secretive. While the agency doesn't release budget or employment figures, many of

its positions are out in the open. Besides operations officers (commonly referred to as spies), the CIA also employs cartographers, statisticians, regional experts, engineers, scientists, linguists, graphic designers, and doctors, among a host of others. The CIA was created in 1947. It offers students internships, co-ops, and graduate study programs. The CIA goes out of its way to get to know those it hires. The hiring process includes a clearance investigation, which, according to the Agency, "addresses comprehensively one's loyalty to the United States, strength of character, trustworthiness, honesty, reliability, discretion, and soundness of judgment. In addition, it examines one's freedom from conflicting allegiances, potential for coercion, and willingness and ability to abide by regulations governing the use, handling and protection of sensitive information."

Department of Homeland Security

Size: 170,000 employees (estimate)
HQ location: Washington, DC
www.dhs.gov

Created in 2003 in the wake of the terrorist attacks of September 11, 2001, the Department of Homeland Security centralizes the management of previously separate government entities including Customs, the Federal Emergency Management Agency (FEMA), the Immigration and Naturalization Service, the Coast Guard, and the Border Patrol. The mission of this department is to secure the safety of the United States. The Department of Homeland Security has taken flack for the confusion inherent in its color-coded "threat level" warning system. (For the record, green means there's a "low" threat level; blue means "guarded"; yellow means there's an "elevated" threat level; orange means "high"; and red means "severe." Since 9/11, we've mostly been at yellow, with a couple of forays into orange.)

Department of State

Size: 28,967 employees; 2002 budget of $15.9 billion
HQ location: Washington, DC
Phone: 202-647-4000
www.state.gov

The State Department operates within the executive branch of government and is the major U.S. foreign policy agency. It hires people in the civil and foreign service sectors and has workers in 180 countries and 43 international organizations. The war on terrorism is currently the department's biggest mission. Other hot-button issues at the Department of State currently include the AIDS epidemic in developing countries and the worldwide slave trade. This is a key department as the U.S. government attempts to increase its influence over the political direction taken by countries in hot spots like the Middle East. Colin Powell is currently the Secretary of State, but there is talk that he'll step aside come the next Presidential election. The Department of State offers student programs and internships for college students hoping to work in foreign affairs.

Environmental Protection Agency (EPA)

Size: 18,000 employees; 2002 budget of $7.3 billion
HQ location: Washington, DC
Phone: 202-260-2080
www.epa.gov

The EPA's work is to protect human health and the environment and to set guidelines for federal, state, and local government. This year the agency celebrated the 30-year anniversary of the Clean Water Act, approved in 1972 so kids could go swimming anywhere, even in the Potomac. Christine Whitman, the former Governor of New Jersey, recently stepped down as head of the

EPA. Many believe Whitman was stuck between a rock and a hard place; Bush administration supporters made it difficult for her to fight to improve the environment, and environmentalists criticized her for inaction. The EPA was created in 1970, and over the years, it has had successes such as the phasing out of the use of leaded gasoline, the passage of the Clean Water Act, and the passage of the Ocean Dumping Ban Act.

Federal Bureau of Investigations (FBI)

Size: 27,000 employees
HQ location: Washington, DC
Phone: 202-324-3000
www.fbi.gov

About one-third of the FBI's employees are stationed in DC—the rest are in its 400 domestic field offices and 40 international locations. According to the FBI, it now accepts special agent applications for just the first seven days of every month—there's no cutoff for other positions, including analysts, linguists, and engineers. The FBI was created in 1908, and over the years, has tackled such cases as the Lindbergh kidnapping and the Brinks robbery and has gone after criminals including Al Capone and Bonnie and Clyde. Today, in response to the events of September 11, 2001, the agency is focusing on protecting the American people from future terrorist attacks. No word on whether there's actually an X-Files department at the FBI.

Government Accounting Office (GAO)

Size: 3,200 employees; 2002 budget of $432 million

HQ location: Washington, DC

Phone: 202-512-3000

www.gao.gov

The GAO is essentially the agency that holds Congress accountable for how it spends U.S. taxpayer dollars. Often called the "watchdog" of Congress, it's independent and non-partisan while trying to help think of ways of making Congress more efficient and responsive. The GAO opened shop in 1921 with the aim of improving federal financial management after World War I costs increased the national debt. This is the department that is designed to question the way the government operates. For instance, even in the current period of pressure to support the war on terrorism in whatever way the U.S. government chooses to wage it, the GAO has criticized the way the U.S. Attorney General has conducted terrorism investigations. The GAO also attempted to take Vice President Cheney to task for refusing to turn over documents relating to U.S. energy policy.

Internal Revenue Service

Size: 96,802 full-time employees; 2003 budget of $9.9 billion

HQ location: Washington, DC

www.irs.gov

The IRS collects federal taxes. It offers many jobs for those in accounting and finance. Accounting grads and professionals can get jobs as IRS agents; IRS agents usually audit individuals or corporations or ensure the compliance of non-profit and government organizations with the tax code. Business and finance grads and professionals can get jobs as IRS officers; IRS officers focus primarily on collecting delinquent taxes. The IRS was created after the 1913

ratification of the 16th Amendment to the U.S. Constitution, which gave Congress the authority to initiate a federal income tax, but its roots go back to the Civil War, when Abraham Lincoln and Congress created the Commissioner of Internal Revenue position and levied an income tax to help pay for the war.

National Aeronautics and Space Administration

Size: 18,918 employees in 2001; 2002 budget of $4.6 billion
HQ location: Washington, DC
www.nasa.gov

These are the people who put man on the moon, as well as developed many technologies that have gone on to become commonplace across American business and society (e.g., microwave technology—as in, the microwave oven in your kitchen). NASA employs scientists, engineers, computer programmers, personnel specialists, accountants, writers, maintenance workers, educators, and people in many other job functions. NASA is currently focused on goals like longer-term space flights and developing new propulsion and optical-communications technologies. NASA was created in 1958 in response to the Soviet Union's launch of the Sputnik satellite, which created fears that the Soviet Union was gaining a strategic advantage over the United States in space.

National Park Service

Size: 20,000 employees plus 90,000 volunteers
HQ location: Washington, DC
www.nps.gov

The National Park Service preserves natural and cultural resources for the enjoyment and education of visitors. The Park Service, which was established in 1916, employs people as park rangers, archaeologists, conservationists,

educators, historic preservationists, park police, and museum staff. Today, National Park sites exist everywhere from Alcatraz in the San Francisco Bay, to Ellis Island in New York Harbor, to Glacier National Park on the border with Canada in Montana, to Big Bend National Park on the border with Mexico in Texas, to Denali National Park and Preserve in Alaska, to Haleakala National Park in Hawaii. The National Park Service, which oversees some 84 million acres of land across the country, played host to more than 421 million visits in 2002.

National Security Agency

Size: undisclosed (20,000-plus estimated employees; 2001 budget estimated at more than $2 billion)
HQ location: Baltimore, MD
www.nsa.gov

The NSA is a top-secret intelligence organization that employs linguists, analysts, mathematicians, and other researchers. While exact figures aren't disclosed, it's apparently one of the largest employers in the state of Maryland and Baltimore Electric's second-largest customer. The organization focuses on signals intelligence (SIGINT) and information systems security (INFOSEC). SIGINT's modern era began during World War II, when U.S. intelligence broke the code used for Japanese military communications, thus allowing the United States to defeat Japan in the Battle of Midway; SIGINT remains a key means of ensuring U.S. security. INFOSEC basically focuses on ensuring the security of classified and sensitive information in American IT and communications systems. The NSA was created in 1952.

Peace Corps

Size: 1,019 employees and 6,678 volunteers; 2003 budget of $295 million
HQ location: Washington, DC
www.peacecorps.gov

Formed by President John F. Kennedy in 1961, the Peace Corps sends volunteers to work in developing countries around the world. Peace Corps volunteers do things like teach English, help establish local businesses, introduce new agricultural techniques, teach environmental awareness, train health workers, and teach people about AIDS awareness and prevention, among other things. The typical Peace Corps stint lasts a little more than two years. Peace Corps alumni enjoy a strong network of fellow alums in all areas of American business and government and the non-profit arena. People working for the Peace Corps include everyone from recent college grads to retirees—though the majority are college grads. The organization is currently on the lookout for people who speak French, people with undergrad or graduate business degrees, teachers of English as a foreign language (TEFL), certified teachers, and people with degrees and/or experience in agriculture, environmental education, and forestry.

The United Nations

Size: 14,000 employees worldwide; 2002 budget of $2.6 billion
HQ location: New York, NY
www.un.org

The UN doesn't fall neatly into the category of either a government or non-profit organization, but it's one of the most visible diplomatic and humanitarian organizations around. It's also notoriously hard to get into—they follow quotas that specify how many people from each member country can be employed in the organization. And until the United States pays its back dues and re-establishes support of some of the UN's missions, the process isn't getting any easier for American applicants.

The website has been newly revamped and now has actual job listings; there are also competitive recruitment exams each fall for young professionals (under the age of 31) for positions in select areas of the organization. Last year's exams focused on the technology, finance, and legal sectors. The UN also hires interpreters, analysts, economists, and program officers.

On the Job

- Non-Profits

- Real People Profiles—Non-Profits

- Government Agencies

- Real People Profiles—Government

Non-Profits

There is no one must-have degree for people wanting to work for a non-profit. While many executive directors have advanced degrees in business, just as many others have backgrounds in public affairs and social sciences. What follows is a listing of typical jobs found at non-profits. Be warned: Positions vary from place to place, so a program director at a small non-profit doesn't necessarily do the same work as a program director at a big organization like the Red Cross.

Executive Director

The grand poobah of the organization, the executive director is the equivalent of a CEO and reports directly to the Board of Directors. He or she is financially accountable for the organization, oversees all strategic planning and management, and may or may not be involved with other duties as well, including, depending on the size of the non-profit, fund-raising and development, board development, hiring of personnel, media relations, program development, and just about anything else that needs to be done.

Salary range: $75,000 and up

Program Director

In larger non-profits and a handful of small ones, a tier of mid-level management is needed. Duties include oversight and management of a specific program, often including hiring personnel, fund-raising, public relations, and all other administrative and management duties specific to the program area. The program director usually reports directly to the executive director.

Salary range: $40,000 to $60,000

Director of Development and Fund-Raising

This job is the mainstay of all non-profit organizations. The development director is responsible for raising the funds necessary to support the organization's budget from a variety of means, which might include writing grant proposals, soliciting government funding, managing direct-mail campaigns and individual donor solicitation, hosting fund-raisers and other events, arranging a fee-for-service-or-product revenue source, and, increasingly, coming up with creative partnerships with businesses.

Salary range: $60,000 to $85,000

Director of Finance and Operations

Manages all accounting and operations, usually including grant administration and often including personnel issues, and serves on the management team. As more non-profits recognize that they cannot maintain public credibility without keeping their own house in scrupulous order, they are hiring CFOs and the like.

Salary range: $40,000 to $60,000

Manager Information Systems

Your typical non-profit is just figuring out what the Internet is and functions on ten-year-old PCs, but hey, you've got to start somewhere. More and more, non-profits are entering the technology age, and if technology is your thing, you can have a huge impact.

Salary range: $45,000 to $60,000

On the Job

Communications Assistant/Director

Depending on the size of the organization, communications may be a more senior or a more junior job. Regardless, duties will usually entail editing and producing a newsletter, managing other communications projects, dealing with the media, and an assortment of public relations activities.

Salary range: $30,000 to $50,000

Program Assistant

Just like it sounds—you'll be doing all of the number-two work on whatever the program is. A notch above administrative help, you'll probably still have to shoulder a fair amount of routine work in addition to trying your hand at more substantive tasks. For the entry-level job seeker, this is a great way to learn about an issue and work closely with your supervisor.

Salary range: $20,000 to $35,000

Event Coordinator

You know this job's for you if you were the first to sign up for Prom Committee in high school, or if you were your fraternity's social chairman. Requires good logistical skills and a mind for getting every last detail correct.

Salary range: $20,000 to $35,000

Director of Volunteers

In non-profits that run on the sweat of volunteer labor, this is a critical, and fun, position. Duties may include recruiting and training volunteers, managing volunteer projects, database management, and related tasks.

Salary range: $25,000 to $45,000

On the Job

Real People Profiles—
Non-Profits

Public Policy Director

Kind of organization: mid-size health and policy non-profit

Years in industry: 7

Years at organization: 5

Education: BA in public policy

Hours per week: 50 to 60

Size of company: 100 employees

Annual salary: $90,000

How often do you travel?

I travel at least twice a month, either to different parts of the state or to Washington. I go to DC at least once a month. There's some international travel, too.

What's the range for starting compensation? Are bonuses handed out?

I'd say about $50,000 to $60,000 for MBAs, while MPPs might get $40,000 to $50,000—no bonuses, no stocks. I started here at $35,000.

Where are the best opportunities for MBAs? For undergrads?

Someone just out of undergraduate school should work for a legislator to get an understanding of policy work. If they don't have policy experience, they could try getting an administrative job in the policy department. MBAs can generally find positions in the accounting and finance departments, and perhaps do assistant controller work. Other positions might be program manager or

On the Job

doing fund-raising work. The most important thing is to have some kind of experience in the sector you're trying to get a position in. If someone hasn't done some kind of policy work, I probably won't hire them.

What's a recent project you worked on?

There's a bill pending before the governor right now on syringe regulation. We worked really hard to get it through the legislature, so that was good. We managed to have good fund-raisers weigh in with the governor and to place lots of op-ed pieces. But it's election year, so . . . (we all know he's going to veto it).

What are some things you most like about working in the non-profit sector?

What I like about my work is more about what I do, being in the policy arena and the mission focus. I like that we're really aimed at helping the world and our community deal with a critical problem. We also have effective management, which is not always the case at a non-profit.

What are some things you (or some people might) dislike about working in the non-profit sector?

No stocks? Maybe that, and the fact that I could make more money somewhere else.

We're facing tough times right now, partly because of the dot-com meltdown. We've had to make cuts because our funding was cut, and that's difficult.

What are the demographics of the organizations you work with? Diversity of ethnicity/gender?

Well, it could be better—we could have more people of color. We're very well-represented in gender and sexual orientation.

Are there other benefits to working at a non-profit such as more vacation time?

In terms of extra benefits, there really aren't bonuses. My organization is generous with vacation time, though. I get 16 hours a month. When I started, it was three weeks per year.

How does the recruiting process work at your organization? What's the best way to get a job there?

We post on opportunitynocs.org and in the local paper and other places online. We don't do any college recruiting. The key is networking and having some background in policy or community work.

What's a typical non-profit career track?

In the smaller non-profits, there is a lot of transition, but for example, our executive director has been here for 15 years.

How would your particular role as public policy director compare to the same role at another organization?

At a smaller organization, they might not have staff, whereas I do.

Describe a typical day.

9:00   Breakfast with state representative of a group working on similar issues.

10:15   Talk with coalition partners about the bill currently before the governor. We need to talk about how they'll react if the governor vetoes the bill.

11:00   Hold a press conference on a recently released report.

1:00   Send reply e-mails to people who've asked my organization to participate in a boycott of a major soft drink company. Then I put calls out to people in the global business community to get their feedback, and see if they support this.

2:30   Staff meeting one-on-one with a policy analyst.

3:15   Plan trip to DC for next week; try to get the plane tickets bought.

4:00   Walk over to the kitchen to eat goodbye cake for someone who's leaving.

7:00   Evening out with staff and state-level colleagues. I'm taking them out to dinner to celebrate the legislative victories we've had this year.

Development Director

Kind of organization: conservation non-profit

Years in industry: 5

Years at organization: 1.5

Hours per week: 45 to 50

Size of company: 13 employees

Annual salary: $62,000

What's your background?

I had volunteer experience in development, so I volunteered for a women's rape crisis center in college. Fund-raising was a part of that work, because it's always a part of that kind of work. I then went into the Peace Corps and wrote three grants for projects that I was working on.

How many days a week do you travel?

I take probably two to three trips a year to the East Coast—DC, New York, Boston.

What is the range for starting compensation for development directors? Necessary background?

The salary is anywhere from $40,000 to $80,000. Development directors are well paid in comparison to other roles. There's no real degree perfect for this work. It's not rocket science, but experience in negotiation and relationship building is important. So much of it is whom you know. You've got the job function, which is great to have experience in, but also the issue you're working on is important. It's also a lot about who you are. There are lots of opportunities out there for the right person.

What's a recent project you worked on?

There are three main areas: individuals, foundations, and corporations (or sponsorships or grants). The person who works with me handles most of our foundations. Once you get a grant, there's a ton of reporting that needs to take place as to what's being done with their money. We put on a fund-raiser, and I spent a lot of time as an event planner for that, including all levels of events production—everything from securing catering and speakers to managing people hosting the tables and producing a film for the event. This was a great example of a team getting together. Hitting our fund-raising goals does fall on my shoulders, but I'm not the only one doing all the talking.

What are some things you most like about working in the non-profit sector?

They're all different—my likes and dislikes have varied according to the organization. The greatest part about my current job is that we apply our vision for the world to our office. The employees get great benefits and extremely long vacations. I also like being surrounded by motivated, passionate people.

What are a few things that you (or some people might) dislike about working in the non-profit sector?

With the commitment that runs so deeply at non-profits, it can mean that people get so entrenched in their work that there's less time for fun and socializing. People devote every minute to making it work. Somewhere in between might be nice.

What are the demographics of the organizations you work with?

We work with five multinationals right now, and our work is focused on building models showing how they can implement sustainability in their organizations. Our work is at the crossroads of non-profit and business. The people who work here mirror that hybrid—we have a higher percentage of people with business backgrounds and scientific backgrounds.

On the Job

How did you get your job?

I knew someone who had consulted with me before, and she brought me here.

What trade publications and/or websites do you recommend?

Chronicle of Philanthropy, the Foundation Center, Compasspoint Non-profit Services, Social Venture Network, and Environmental Grantmakers Association.

Describe a typical day.

8:00 Bike to work.

8:20 Arrive at the office; find two voice mails. One from a prospective donor with whom I was supposed to have lunch. She has to postpone the introductory conversation for the third time.

8:45 Continue the editing process on a $55 million endowment proposal that we need to submit by the end of the week. This proposal will be submitted to an individual, which makes the writing process more difficult. There are no guidelines—the whole thing is based on building relationships.

10:20 Flurry of e-mail checking and responding.

10:30 Go to my weekly meeting with the associate development director and the executive director. We go through upcoming deadlines and projects as well of a laundry list of people who need to be contacted or cultivated within the week. We have a call with the fund-raising committee of the board this week and need to prep for it and there is an East Coast trip to meet with funders next week. So we do some review on whom we'll be going to meet with and when.

12:00 Bike to an hour-long yoga class, come back to the office to heat up the leftovers I brought for lunch.

1:25 Check and respond to e-mails.

1:30 Call the board member of a nationwide workplace giving campaign that focuses on environmental causes.

3:00 Do some prospecting research on a certain technology CEO who has expressed an interest in getting involved with our work.

3:15	Meet briefly with a volunteer and our director of operations about the imminent database migration that's happening in the office.
3:30	Report via phone to a funder on a local technology and sustainability initiative for which they have provided seed funding. Their three-year funding commitment of $120,000 is helping us to get the project off the ground. As is the case with most foundations, they also have rigorous reporting requirements so as to measure their social return on investment.
4:30	Meet with the director of communications to discuss our donor communications through the end of the year. This includes e-mails, face-to-face meetings, mailings, and events.
6:00	Head to a nearby presentation on investments in renewable energy.
7:30	Bike home.

Development Director

Kind of organization: environmental non-profit

Age: 27

Years in business: 2

Education: BA

Hours per week: 40 to 50

Size of company: 20 employees

Annual salary: $40,000

What do you do?

I'm the development director at a national non-profit environmental organization. We work with large corporations to help them integrate social and environmental priorities into their strategy.

I am responsible for meeting our budgetary needs, which come to approx. $1.4 million each year. One-fourth of that comes from earned income (paid to us by our clients), one-fourth comes from individuals, and a little less than half comes from private foundation grants. A very small percentage comes from corporate gifts, sponsorships, and government grants.

How did you get your job?

I used to work with the VP of Operations in my previous job. When the Development Director job opened up, she contacted me to see if I'd be interested.

What are your career aspirations?

I'd like to work jointly in the fields of private investment and environmental change.

What kind of person does well in your job?

A person who likes to talk to people, who likes to get people excited about ideas, and who doesn't mind being associated with the money side of social change work (no pun intended).

What do you like most about your job?

I like the fact that I get to help drive resources toward positive change. I also like connecting donors with the change that they are able to effect in the world by donating their money. When philanthropy is effective, it benefits the donor as well as the recipient, and it's very empowering to facilitate that connection.

What do you like least?

I don't like the power inequity in traditional donor/grantee relationships. That is to say, I'd rather that contributions and grants established a partnership of equals. Instead, it can feel like the usual rich/poor better-than-thou relationship.

I don't like that directors of development (DoDs) often get shafted in terms of respect. Since the work is primarily about money, traditional organizations tend to marginalize DoDs into a non-programmatic role, kind of like sales. This doesn't make a ton of sense, especially because the DoD is often the person in touch with funders and can be a helpful voice in packaging great programs.

What misconceptions do people have about your job?

Again, people often think of DoDs as mere salespeople. Also, people commonly think that development directors are individually responsible for raising an organization's money. In fact, it is the role of all non-profit workers to represent the organization with funders, especially the executive director. The DoD often just facilitates the meetings.

On the Job

What would you have done differently in your career?

I would have become better friends with our board of directors, both to raise money directly from them and to make useful connections for my future career.

How can someone get a job like yours?

Work in grantwriting or development consulting. Directors of development are often hired internally. Either that, or make friends with a well-placed hiring manager who can bring you in from the outside.

Describe a typical day.

8:00   Catch the bus to the office.

8:45   Drink a cup of tea while checking e-mails and phone messages.

9:00   Attend a board development committee call to discuss the month's planned development activities, goals, and major gifts and grants to finalize.

11:00   Spend some time writing a grant for a large multiyear public grant from the Environmental Protection Agency.

12:30   Lunch with coworkers. It's a beautiful day, so we eat our sandwiches in a nearby park.

1:30   Work on internal program development for a corporate climate change initiative. Today I'm gathering information for a brochure designed to "sell" the idea of the initiative.

4:00   Phone call with the executive director and foundation program officer about an upcoming grant deadline and whether we should submit a proposal.

5:00   Thank-you calls and e-mails to individual donors to our organization.

6:30   Head home.

Government Agencies

Because there are thousands upon thousands of government positions, from park rangers to legislative aides, we've broken down the job descriptions into major service- and policy-oriented categories, followed by a position or two that you'd most commonly find in the sector.

Note: Government jobs move across a set pay scale that is fairly wide in range and depends on the candidate's experience. Theoretically, all positions could incorporate ten grades or more, which would translate into a salary range of $35,000 to $75,000 across the board. (See "Compensation" in "The Workplace" chapter for more information.)

Capitol Hill

Generally speaking, this refers to the House, Senate, and related staff. Positions include staff assistant, legislative correspondent, legislative assistant, press secretary, and legislative director. These positions are usually located in Washington, DC, but senators and representatives also have home offices. People with some expertise also serve on committees and subcommittees.

Legislative Aide

One of the most common positions on Capitol Hill, this is a relatively mid-level position, which you can get after working as a staff assistant or legislative correspondent. Aides are responsible for finding out everything there is to know about a particular issue, and then brief other staff members. Aides often meet with interest groups and talk to constituents—it's definitely a "people" position.

Press Secretary

"Getting the word out"—that's the primary responsibility of a press secretary (or communications director). Press secretaries, who are the office's media liaison, draft a Member's speeches and statements, and write press releases and other statements.

Development

From your local health and human services department to federal agencies such as the Agency for International Development (USAID), development agencies provide economic assistance to the people or region they serve. These agencies hire budget analysts, medical personnel, caseworkers, program directors, and technology professionals, among others.

Program Officer

Program officers generally act as advisers to their directors, and help implement the particular project. This position is one of the main generalist jobs at a development agency, whether local or federal.

Diplomacy

Diplomatic work often involves "being the face of America to the world." The field definitely has more nuances to it than this—in addition to implementing U.S. policy, diplomatic work involves creating policy, assessing the image the country has abroad, and doing more administrative consular work. This is generally a State Department job, including all foreign service officers and specialists. Most people in the professional corps (rather than the administrative corps) are career foreign service employees, and the five foreign service "cones" are economic, political, consular, public diplomacy, and administrative.

Foreign Service Officer

The work varies depending on the cone. Junior officers are required to spend some time in each before fully moving to their specific area, so they have a broad understanding about embassy and diplomatic work. "Career" foreign service officers are the senior corps, and contrary to what you might think, about 70 percent of all ambassadors are career, and not presidential, appointees.

Economics

The Government Accounting Office (GAO) and the Congressional Budget Office (CBO) are two of the most important economic agencies on the federal level. Local and federal governments employ thousands of accountants, auditors, economists, analysts, and statisticians in their ongoing quest to manage the budget, fund programs, and make economic projections.

Budget Analyst

This is a good role for number crunchers. Analysts review proposed budgets and provide advice and recommendations. Analysts do a lot of data review with their team and write reports detailing their findings. This is generally a position that requires an advanced degree, such as an MBA or PhD.

Assistant Director

At the more senior level, assistant directors manage and direct project teams or divisions. Experience in analyzing policy issues is often required, as is experience in presenting, explaining, and defending your group's recommendations.

Environment

Environmental agencies such as the EPA work to implement national guidelines for water safety, clean air, wildlife and wilderness preservation, and more. Besides

the obvious need for scientists, the agency also needs computer technicians, public affairs officers, and people who can work in its legal department.

Environmental Protection Specialist

This is essentially an analyst position that helps the local or federal agency comply with any environmental regulation (pollution, recycling). The experience level ranges for this position, and duties can include writing reports, giving presentations, and analyzing data.

Security

There are a vast number of agencies doing security work, which deals with everything from national readiness and bioterrorism to border control. The FBI, CIA, and the NSA are the most "visible" agencies, but other security agencies include the INS, the Coast Guard, the Food and Drug Administration (FDA), and the U.S. Customs Service. There's currently a push to hire mathematicians, statisticians, linguists, and analysts at all levels, and with the development of the new Homeland Security Department, this is one of the hottest—and most controversial—areas of government. One intelligence recruiter says that the "trend right now is in foreign languages, and also in business and engineering positions."

Intelligence Analyst

Analysts assess current events by collecting research on classified and open information, and use state-of-the-art toys to do their work. There is a lot of oral and written report making, and analysts often have a background in technology and communications.

Electronic Technician

This is essentially like a systems administration position. Technicians install and maintain all communications systems and relevant databases and often oversee a team of junior technicians. This position is generally offered to people with one to two years of specialized experience.

Real People Profiles— Government

Legislative Director

Type of organization: state assemblyperson's office

Years in industry: 4

Education: BA in Asian-American Studies; MA in Public Policy

Size of organization: 8 employees

Annual salary: $55,000

How did you get your job?

I was working in another assembly office when my assemblyperson was elected. She had her office call me after she was elected, and now I work there. I've been in state legislature for four years now.

What did you do before?

I was a lobbyist for about six years before working in legislation. I started as a student—I was active with student government at the university, and then my first job out of school was as a lobbyist for a university student association.

What are some of the positives of working where you do?

It's very rewarding when you're able to get good legislation passed, and you get to work on a whole array of issues. It's also fun—every day is different, and you meet lots of different people.

What are some of the drawbacks?

Well, there's a lot of strategic compromising. Legislators will often refuse to vote on your bill for political reasons, not because they don't support the bill. This is very frustrating.

What kind of career path do you see for yourself?

That's a good question. I guess I'll stay until the assemblywoman is termed out, and then perhaps go to another member that I support. Sometimes people go into lobbying after doing this kind of work.

What would you recommend for someone who wants to do this kind of work?

There's really no specific degree that you need—it doesn't really matter. If someone hasn't done legislative work before, I really recommend getting an internship or networking with people who do the job. Sometimes jobs like this are posted, but often it's by word of mouth.

Describe a typical day.

9:00   Arrive at the assemblyperson's office, and start answering and returning calls, which we get throughout the day.

9:20   Check the assemblyperson's schedule for the day and check e-mail.

9:30   Check in with assemblyperson on bills she has to present in committees that day.

10:00   Work on talking points for the assemblyperson for a bill she has to present in committee.

11:00   Meet with constituents who are at the Capitol for their annual Lobby Day.

11:30   Make calls to other assembly members' offices about our bill that their bosses will be voting on, and try to secure their votes.

1:30   Monitor a policy committee that's beginning its hearing.

3:00   Run to wherever the assemblyperson is (she could be anywhere!) and bring her to the committee hearing where she has to present her bill. I'll give her last-minute updates and points—this process can take anywhere from 15 minutes to two hours.

4:00   Attend a staff briefing on a hearing the assemblyperson sits on for the next day.

6:00   Start preparing talking points for the next day's hearing.

Economist/Analyst

Type of organization: government accounting group
Years at organization: 1
Education: PhD in economics
Size of organization: 3,000 employees
Annual salary: $65,000

How would you describe the culture at your organization?

Well, we like to joke about how we're the anal, careful, detail-oriented types—the critical thinkers. But our office is much more casual than the head DC office. The culture really depends on the field office.

How many hours do you work a week?

About 45 to 50, but I don't really have to. People work less than that without a problem.

How often do you travel?

I only travel about 5 percent of the year, though it's more typical of people in my organization to travel about 25 percent, mostly to the East Coast. We have an international branch that travels about 50 percent.

What's the compensation range? At what level do people enter the organization?

For the non-administrative jobs, you have to have some kind of graduate degree—because we're analysts here. A PhD economist might come in at the GS-12 rate, while MBAs might be GS-11. There are good perks—we have an awards system that's linked to our performance, paid out in either vacation time or money. Because we start with such little vacation time, that's how I'm taking mine. There is also the option of having some of your student loans paid off, up to about $3,000 per year.

How is the organization set up, in terms of major divisions, groups, and locations?

Our buzzword is "matrix" here—we have several different groups, but using this matrix system, groups can work on overlapping issues. We work in teams that are responsible for different industries. There's one team that works on tax and justice, for example. In terms of location, the main office is in DC with several field offices throughout the country.

What's a recent project you've worked on?

The way it works is that we get a request letter from Congress asking for research on a certain issue. If the organization accepts the request, it gets assigned to the appropriate team. One person takes charge of what's called the design phase, which is followed by a phase in which we map out everything that's feasible, then come up with a commitment date for when we'll release the report. It's considered really important for us to stick to our dates. The last report I worked on, our recommendations were adopted, so that was a success.

What are some things you like about your work?

I love working on issues that concern Congress, and writing reports that are actually read and impact policy.

What are some of the things you dislike?

Government vacation time—it's really low initially. And a lot of the paperwork is unnecessary.

Describe a typical day.

8:00   Arrive at work, log on, and check e-mail.

8:10   Load SAS and begin preparing large data set for analysis.

8:15   Return call from team member in DC regarding questions on analysis.

8:30   Resume SAS programming.

8:35	Address a colleague's question regarding the appropriate use of language describing sampling errors in a report.
8:45	Meet with supervisee to review his work for the past two days, and to provide feedback.
9:15	Resume SAS programming.
10:30	Prepare documentation for annual performance review.
12:00	Hot lunch date!
1:00	Programming again.
2:30	Monthly feedback meeting with my supervisee to get his perspectives on the organization and to answer his questions about our work.
3:30	More programming . . .
4:15	Phone meeting with former PhD colleague who's applying to the World Bank—she wants application advice.
4:45	You guessed it—programming!
5:30	Homeward bound.

The Workplace

- Lifestyle and Culture

- Hours

- Workplace Diversity

- Compensation

- Travel

- Perks

- Vacations

- Career Path

- Insider Scoop

WetFeet®

Lifestyle and Culture

The lifestyle in any non-profit, no matter how entrepreneurial, is going to be decidedly "un-corporate." It might, however, be quite similar to working for a start-up business. You'll find that your work is inherently integrated with your values and those of the organization—in a field that is driven by mission, vision, and ideals, you can't escape it!

On the flip side, the work environment in a government position will be much more formal. "Casual" dress means that men might not have to wear a tie. Generally speaking, the environment in DC is stuffier than in other locations. But as in a non-profit, you'll find yourself surrounded by people who are dedicated to their work in the same way that you are. A note on culture in federal offices: The tenor of the workplace can change when administrations change. For instance, one federal government insider tells us that her office is more formal under the Bush administration than it was under the Clinton administration and that she has to do more frequent paperwork due to tighter oversight of her department by higher-ups. And if you worked for the Immigration and Naturalization Service, for instance, you would probably have experienced some shifting of the cultural sands when the Service was absorbed into the new Department of Homeland Security alongside Customs, the Border Patrol, and other formerly separate organizations.

Hours

Generally speaking, most people in non-profits work 50-plus hours per week—and often log the odd hours: weekends, late nights before big events, or on deadline. The upside is, because these groups usually have more casual work environments than a corporate office, you can often set your own hours—as long as the work gets done. One note of caution: Burnout is a big factor in this sector, because so many passionate types push themselves so hard in their quest to "save the world." There's always more work to be done. The better-managed non-profits recognize that you need to have a life outside of work, no matter how much you love your job.

People working in government positions tend to enjoy a more traditional 40- to 45-hour workweek, though the hours will go up when reports are due or some other deadline is looming.

Workplace Diversity

It's difficult to make generalizations about workplace diversity in government and non-profits. If you work in a big city for a big government agency, for instance, your workplace is likely to be far more diverse than many corporation's workplaces. But if you work in rural Arizona for the Border Patrol, while your coworkers are likely to reflect the local ethnic mix, odds are good that most of them are going to be fairly conservative, law-and-order types, and you won't fit in if you're a New Ager, for example.

And while many non-profits have highly diverse staffs, often, because of their missions, they're going to be fairly homogenous in terms of the political views of staffers. For instance, you're going to have a hard time finding pro-life coworkers if you work for Planned Parenthood, or gun-control advocates at the National Rifle Association. Both sectors inherently place a larger emphasis on diversity than corporate America in general, though—the government, to mirror society as a whole, and non-profits, because they often serve the disadvantaged and are staffed by people who have chosen careers outside the corporate American mainstream.

Compensation

If anything, low compensation is the biggest drawback to working in the non-profit sector. Then again, it does tend to act as a filter and weed out those who aren't truly motivated and dedicated. One insider recalls a graduating MBA student who was all ready to "go out and save the world, and then he had a hissy fit when he found out what they were going to pay him." Be forewarned, you will probably make at least a third less than you could at a comparable for-profit job. Executive directors usually make from $40,000 to $70,000, but those working for large, national non-profits can make upwards of $90,000—especially in New York and Washington, DC. Just don't expect to get those jobs without a lot of experience.

Entry-level positions are even more salary-challenged. For an undergraduate starting at a non-profit, expect to make from $20,000 to $35,000, depending on work experience and title. Most employees starting out with an organization can expect to pay their dues for a year or two—but if they do, they're likely to be promoted from within.

Compensation for federal government positions can seem complex at first. To understand it, first you must understand that there are two basic classes of jobs in the federal government. One is the competitive civil service; most government jobs are civil service jobs; these are subject to civil service laws governing hiring and pay. The second comprises excepted service jobs; agencies employing excepted service employees set their own hiring and pay standards. Some agencies including the FBI and the CIA have only excepted service employees; others may have employees in both federal classes.

White-collar competitive civil service positions are given a GS (general scale) ranking. There are multiple steps within each grade, so that you could be a GS-12, step 4, for example. This is the base salary—locality adjustments can increase the salary by 20 to 25 percent. And some hires can get special recruitment and/or relocation bonuses. Similarly, some employees can get special retention bonuses. Don't expect to enjoy these financial perks, though—they're not very common. In addition, some federal jobs can pay significantly higher rates than the base, if they're located somewhere particularly remote or the job is particularly undesirable, or if the prevailing local market rate for people in those positions is especially high compared to general scale compensation (e.g., doctors, engineers, and some IT folks).

Entry-level jobs for those with a bachelor's degree are usually in the GS-5 to GS-8 range. Those with a master's degree or some directly related job experience generally start in the range of grades GS-9 to GS-12. Following are salary tables from the U.S. Office of Personnel Management detailing current federal civil service compensation (including a few tables for some of the regions where the pay is higher than the base pay for each GS level). (Note: There are additional pay schedules for certain executive-level federal employees, as well as key federal scientific and professional employees. Also, federal law enforcement employees receive somewhat higher compensation at each GS ranking than other federal employees.)

2003 General Schedule of Federal Employment Salaries

Grade (GS)	Salary ($)									
	Step 1	Step 2	Step 3	Step 4	Step 5	Step 6	Step 7	Step 8	Step 9	Step 10
1	15,214	15,722	16,228	16,731	17,238	17,536	18,034	18,538	18,559	19,031
2	17,106	17,512	18,079	18,559	18,767	19,319	19,871	20,423	20,975	21,527
3	18,664	19,286	19,908	20,530	21,152	21,774	22,396	23,018	23,640	24,262
4	20,952	21,650	22,348	23,046	23,744	24,442	25,140	25,838	26,536	27,234
5	23,442	24,223	25,004	25,785	26,566	27,347	28,128	28,909	29,690	30,471
6	26,130	27,001	27,872	28,743	29,614	30,485	31,356	32,227	33,098	33,969
7	29,037	30,005	30,973	31,941	32,909	33,877	34,845	35,813	36,781	37,749
8	32,158	33,230	34,302	35,374	36,446	37,518	38,590	39,662	40,734	41,806
9	35,519	36,703	37,887	39,071	40,255	41,439	42,623	43,807	44,991	46,175
10	39,115	40,419	41,723	43,027	44,331	45,635	46,939	48,243	49,547	50,851
11	42,976	44,409	45,842	47,275	48,708	50,141	51,574	53,007	54,440	55,873
12	51,508	53,225	54,942	56,659	58,376	60,093	61,810	63,527	65,244	66,961
13	61,251	63,293	65,335	67,377	69,419	71,461	73,503	75,545	77,587	79,629
14	72,381	74,794	77,207	79,620	82,033	84,446	86,859	89,272	91,685	94,098
15	85,140	87,978	90,816	93,654	96,492	99,330	10,2168	10,5006	10,7844	110,682

Source: U.S. Office of Personnel Management.

The Workplace

Travel

Contrary to what you might expect, there are actually a fair number of non-profits that require at least moderate travel, and in some cases, extensive. Generally speaking, your small grassroots non-profit won't necessarily fit this bill. But larger non-profits, particularly those national groups with local chapters or other affiliates, may require a fair amount of travel, depending on your job description. Executive directors and development directors may be required to fly to meet with funders if under consideration for a grant. And they are continually looking for networking opportunities near and far to meet these funders in person and pitch their program. Additionally, there is a sizable conference circuit in the sector—ongoing meetings about "best practices" and sectorwide issues that provide opportunities to network and compare notes with other organizations.

Government jobs can also provide significant travel opportunities. Foreign service officers get to spend the majority of their careers overseas, and large federal agencies with national field offices will require employees to come to the head office from time to time. On the state level, lobbyists and legislative aides can make trips to the capital and around the area where they're working.

Perks

Many non-profit employees consider travel one of the biggest perks (it can be quite competitive deciding who gets to attend a conference in Hawaii, e.g.). Other perks include interaction with well-known public figures, including corporate CEOs, politicians, and other important community members.

For government employees, the perks include a wide array of parties and functions as well as opportunities to mingle with "powerful" people. Many agencies also have flexible time schedules, allowing employees to work less than five days a week. People with student loans will be happy to know that most agencies will help competitive civil servants repay student loans, up to around $6,000 per year—tax-free.

Vacations

There is no hard and fast rule about vacation in the non-profit sector. Some organizations follow policies similar to those in the business world—two weeks a year, plus holidays. However, many non-profits recognize that their employees work long, hard hours for lower pay and choose to compensate them in other ways. It's not unusual for a non-profit to offer three to four weeks of vacation a year. Again, because the work environment is usually less formal in this sector, many non-profits are understanding and flexible about taking the occasional day

off—particularly if you perform well and are on top of all your work. Some even go so far as to require employee "wellness" days in order to prevent burnout.

Government organizations tend to give skimpy vacation time, but can make up for it in other ways. When starting, two weeks per year for the first few years is normal, and then it increases gradually after that. The good thing is that many agencies offer rewards and performance bonuses that can be taken as either money or vacation time, and also allow flexible work schedules. One insider we talked to, a lawyer who's been working for the Department of Health and Human Services for around five years, has more than two months of vacation time stored up, and can't take enough time away from the office to get rid of it. For him, the frequent, lengthy vacations he can take more than compensate for the fact that his salary is significantly lower than it would be in private practice.

Career Path

A typical career path at a non-profit is, well, not typical. People move around quite a bit in these organizations, and where they go depends on the position they started with. Moving from a program director to a director of development is more of a lateral move, and not uncommon. This level is excellent for people who like to be in the thick of things—roles tend to be more managerial further up the ladder. An executive director generally has many years of experience and excellent contacts within the field, as well as considerable management experience—he or she is just as likely to come from outside the organization as from the inside.

Government career paths tend to be more defined—once you're in, you can count on a lot of job stability and a predictable schedule of promotions. Very rarely do people go below their current GS ranking—promotions move on a regulated, vertical scale. Many federal agencies have reciprocal agreements with other agencies, so if you want to move from the foreign service into the USAID, for example, it would be a relatively easy transition to make. Many government employees eventually go into advisory or research roles at think tanks, such as the Brookings Institute or the Heritage Foundation, or into the private sector as advisors or even as educators.

How Non-Profit and Government Careers Compare to Careers in Business

The following generalizations will help you quickly and easily compare non-profit careers, government careers, and corporate careers by rating careers in these arenas in a number of important categories:

Business vs. Government vs. Non-Profit Careers

Category	Business	Government	Non-Profit
Compensation	Highest	Middle	Lowest
Hours	Highest	Lowest	Middle
Amount of bureaucracy	Some	Lots	Little
Pace of work	Fastest	Slowest	Middle
Amount of management oversite of employees	Some	High	Low
Diversity of responsibilities	Some	Low	High
Job security	Low	High	Medium

The Workplace

Insider Scoop

What Employees Really Like about Non-Profits

Living your passion. "You get to be who you are, not just what you do," says one non-profit insider. In other words, people working in this field find that they can fully live their values. Their work isn't so much work as it is a passion or a calling.

It's the people. You will be working with great people. "The people I work with are bright and committed," says one director of a non-profit. A common sentiment voiced by all of the insiders, who welcome the opportunity to be surrounded by passionate, like-minded individuals.

The only rule is . . . You will be making up the rules as you go. While that might not sound good to someone who wants a lot of structure in his or her job, it's great for self-motivated, committed people—people who love the flexibility to apply their best ideas in order to get things done.

The downward-facing dog of workplaces. A flexible work environment is one of the most appealing things at non-profits. Many of these organizations are less hierarchical, bureaucratic, and structured than their private-sector counterparts. One insider says that her organization brings "the kind of environment we're trying to promote" into the workplace—one that relies on independent self-starters managing their own time, rather than clockwatchers worried about face time.

You own this job. You will have a lot of responsibility and ownership of your work. One of the great things about non-profit work is that in these sometimes small and under-resourced organizations, every hand on deck counts.

What Employees Really Like about Government

I wrote that report! Though government can work at a glacial pace, insiders say that one of the best things about working in the industry is knowing your work is having an impact. You may not see that impact right away, but all in due time . . .

Once you're in, you're in. There is a tremendous amount of job security in government positions, and people can have long, exacting careers without much fear of losing their job. There can be a flip side, however (see "Watch Out!" following).

Power, up close and personal. The chance to meet policy-makers, legislators, maybe even heads of state is a major plus. If you're someone who likes to network, you'll have plenty of opportunities.

40 hours and not a minute more. Most government employees work plain old 40-hour workweeks, and love that fact—and the fact that they're compensated if they have to work longer hours.

Non-Profits: Watch Out!

You call THAT a paycheck? Low pay is typically the number-one gripe. If your heart is where the money is, then you may want to think twice about working for a non-profit. Your passion for the cause you're working for has to more than compensate for the low paycheck for you to be happy in the non-profit arena.

Burnout. One insider says that there's so much to do with so few resources. That, combined with the frenetic pace of people working so hard towards a particular goal, can make for a "hothouse" environment.

Because the founder says so. Some of the typical dysfunctions in a non-profit can include lack of clear accountability, confusion over roles and responsibilities, a dictatorial founder, poor management, and the never-ending funding crises.

The Workplace

Living a life of luxury . . . not! "Cash-strapped" is an adjective that can be used to describe many non-profits. As a result, don't be surprised if you find yourself getting green with envy when your friends in business describe their nifty corporate intranets, and their convenient car-service rides home when they work late, and their free cappuccinos every morning, and . . . you get the idea.

Government: Watch Out!

No month-long trip to the Riviera. You do get vacation time, of course, but it can be a few years before you move up to even three weeks off per year. But how would you pay for this trip, anyway? The familiar complaint: low salaries.

Paperwork, paperwork. No one seems to be able to explain just why this is, and insiders use words like "bloated," "redundant," and "insane" to describe some of the bureaucratic chores they have to do. Process is paramount, and even a simple proposal might need multiple reviews and sign-offs.

Didn't I see you here 20 years ago? Government jobs are pretty stable, and some people would like to coast as long as possible, while putting in minimal work. This is not standard by any means, but insiders say that there sometimes seems to be a little "extra weight" in the boat.

Politics. No matter how good your proposal is or how obviously important the issue is, at one time or another you'll have to make some distasteful compromises. One insider working on an assemblyperson's staff says that seeing people voting against certain bills because of election year politics is one of the most disillusioning parts of her work.

Getting Hired

- The Recruiting Process

- Interviewing Tips

- Getting Grilled

- Grilling Your Interviewer

The Recruiting Process

Non-Profits

Finding and landing your dream job in a non-profit may take some effort on your part. Unlike the private sector, non-profits are neither large enough, nor financially endowed enough, to come looking for you. There are no formal recruiting structures set up. Rather, non-profits rely on the energy and efforts of you, the job seeker. However, some informal—but tried and true—ways of getting your foot in the door are available to you.

Network. Landing a great job often depends more on whom rather than what you know. Many non-profits hire future employees out of a circle of folks already working in their community—for another non-profit or as a volunteer. So go to conferences, meet people, and get involved! Don't forget to use your alumni and peer networks as well—your friends in the private sector would make great board members for non-profits.

Conduct informational interviews. Uncertain which issue you want to focus on? Get out and talk to people in a variety of organizations until you find the area that piques your interest. Generally speaking, folks in this sector are "people" people and will be glad to help if you show interest and enthusiasm.

Volunteer. This is perhaps the most important way to get your foot in the door with any non-profit—and usually the starting point for gaining experience in the sector. Once you've found an organization you'd like to work for—or even one that is similar—sign on as a volunteer, even if they're not hiring immediately. Many non-profits rely on volunteers to do a variety of important tasks. You'll

learn more about an issue area, gain skills, add to your resume, make new friends, and feel great in the process. And you just might land that paid job when something opens up.

Intern. Spending a few months as an intern in a non-profit (either paid or unpaid) is a great way to gain experience, see whether you like working for a non-profit, and get your foot in the door. Especially if most of your work experience is in the private sector, doing a summer internship is a great trial run. Likewise, if all of your experience is in the non-profit sector, you may consider a summer internship in a business, just to add to your repertoire of skills when you go back into the non-profit environment.

Government

Most government agencies have dedicated recruiters who attend college career fairs, industry conferences, and other job placement events. Recruiters tend to be regionally located, and look for candidates who have the particular set of skills their area needs. One intelligence agency recruiter says that while many people like giving a resume to someone face to face, resumes submitted online or by mail go through the same process as those given to recruiters directly. So try your luck on agency websites. Government agencies will have recruiting "blitzes," too—security agencies are recruiting year-round right now, while other agencies such as the GAO accept applications only at certain times of the year.

Also, because a huge number of government employees will be retiring in the next ten to 15 years, there's a lot of advancement potential.

Exams. There are required competitive exams for some government positions, especially in the State Department. The foreign service written exam is probably the largest. It's given several times a year around the country and is taken by thousands of people. If you pass, you'll be invited to an oral assessment.

Some form of security clearance is required for most government positions, but unless you're going to need top-secret clearance, the process is minimal. Agencies that require extensive background investigations include the State Department, FBI, CIA, and NSA. These investigations can take several months, prolonging the hiring process.

Network. As in the non-profit sector, whom you know can be very important. If an agency gets flooded with anonymous e-mailed resumes, it helps to have yours as close to the top of the pile as possible. Also, government HR agencies tend to be very rigid when it comes to the "minimum requirements" needed for a position. If you can get your resume in through someone you know, you can avoid the by-the-numbers screening process.

Volunteer. If you're looking to work in a legislator's office or to help with a campaign, volunteering can be the best way to get your foot in the door. Free help is never declined, and the exposure you get by going to fund-raisers, handing out literature, doing research, and making phone calls will be extremely useful once a position does open up.

Intern. There are hundreds of internships available in different branches of the government, the majority for students, including the Presidential Management Intern Program and the White House Fellows Program. Most of these are paid and last three to four months (though some are more like fellowships, and can last one to two years). Individual agency websites have a lot of information, so be sure to check with them. Also, a pretty comprehensive list of internships can be found at http://www.usajobs.opm.gov/.

Interviewing Tips

Non-Profits

1. **Do your homework.** It's a good idea to look at an organization's website and download a copy of its annual report, or call ahead and ask for one. You can tell a lot about an organization from its mission statement, the language used in its literature, and its public image. The annual report (or equivalent) should give you a glimpse of the inner workings of the non-profit, with detailed information on annual budget, program areas, board members, and the like. Also consider obtaining local news clippings about the group in your library. And if the non-profit runs a business, be sure to test its product or services as a consumer.

2. **Talk to people who work there, and who know what the issues are.** This is crucial. If you've never worked in education reform, but desperately want that job at a local charter school, you must convince your interviewer why you care about education. Several insiders say, "You'd be amazed at how often people don't have the slightest idea about what we're working on." Read articles in the mainstream media or any new books on the topic, and emphasize the skills that you bring to the job.

3. **Think about why you want this job and why it makes sense in the progression of your career.** The more you have thought concretely about your interests, skills, and values, the more articulate you will be. Be honest and direct in the interview. Many non-profits desperately need more employees with management skills. Talk frankly about your relevant work experience, education, and all the skills you can bring to the job. Just be careful not to oversell yourself.

4. **Dress the part.** In non-profits, the dress code can vary widely. Even if your interviewer shows up in jeans or even shorts, you should be dressed professionally, without being too corporate. Try a nice pantsuit, or skirt and jacket ensemble that is classy without being intimidating. Khakis and a nice jacket are fine for guys. Use sound judgment: What is appropriate at a national non-profit in Washington, DC, might be overdressed for a grassroots, community-based organization on the West Coast.

Government

1. **Again, do your homework.** By the time you're called in for an interview, you'll have had a lot of time to prepare, so take advantage of it. The interviewing process is complex and pretty formal—chances are that you'll have to go through a series of interviews with different people and through several rounds of approval. As there can be a lag time between interviews, try to assess what you've learned from your first interviews and bring that knowledge with you to later ones. Just about all government agencies have websites with mission statements and project descriptions—look at them.

2. **Talk to recruiters about what the agency needs now.** Recruiters are surprisingly easy to find—most agencies will tell you when and where they're going to be doing recruiting in your area. And then talk to someone who works in the organization. Contact people you know to see if there are openings. While major agencies post their listings, smaller offices like those of an assemblyperson or local legislator might only post internally.

3. **Be candid in your interview.** You may have to go through a standard HR interview before you see someone related to the position you're trying to get. Often HR is looking for plain facts more than they are assessing you as a person. Make sure they know just how perfectly you suit the position,

and bring your resume with you. For positions requiring a background investigation, answer all questions as frankly as possible—it will help streamline the hiring process.

4. **Play it safe with what you wear.** Government employees, especially on the national or federal level, tend to dress conservatively. You don't have to throw style out the window, but know that pantsuits and skirts are the norm for women, and that your male interviewer will probably be wearing a tie. Once you're in, you can assess your particular office's dress code, but it's best to play it safe until then.

Getting Grilled

Some interviewers work from a script, others wing it, and still others tailor their questions to your particular background. Here are some things they might ask:

- Why do you want to work in this non-profit/government agency? (Definitely talk about your passion for service work here, but try to speak about your passion for the specific mission of the potential employer, as well, using examples of your longstanding interest in this particular cause or mission.)

- Where do you see yourself five or ten years down the road? (If it's in a more advanced position with the employer, fine. Otherwise, think about how the employer organization and the position you're interviewing for fit logically into a career roadmap that connects where you are currently with where you plan to be, careerwise, in five or ten years.)

- Give me an example of a time you took on a leadership role.

- Give me an example of a time you worked as part of a team to achieve a common goal.

- For non-profit opportunities: Are you flexible in your work style and able to play a variety of roles to get projects done? (Think of specific examples that will illuminate your flexibility.)

- For government jobs: Are you able to deal with bureaucracy?

- If you're coming from a business background: Are you prepared to deal with a significantly different culture, one based on a mission statement of service to clients or citizens rather than on profits?

Grilling Your Interviewer

Here are some good questions to ask your interviewer. Not all of them may apply to you, but most are of general interest to anyone choosing an employer, and we have listed some of special importance to both government and non-profit candidates. The questions assume you will have already covered basic topics like compensation and benefits packages.

Non-Profits

- What are the organization's most impressive achievements? (You should already have a pretty good grasp of at least part of the answer to this question, and have exhibited that fact.)
- How would you describe the culture of the organization?
- What are the organization's major goals for the next few years? How does the organization measure success? How does the organization reward success?
- How do you think this organization will change in the next ten years?
- What kind of person does well in this organization?
- What have some people in this position gone on to do in their careers?

Government

- How would you describe this agency's culture?
- How do you think this agency will change in the next ten years?
- Do people tend to make their careers in this agency, or do they tend to move to other agencies or into the private sector? What have some people in this position gone on to do in their careers?
- What kind of person does well in this agency?

- What are the agency's major goals for the next few years? How does the agency measure success?

- What are your favorite/least favorite things about working for this agency?

For Your Reference

- Recommended Reading

- Other Resources

Recommended Reading

The Natural Step for Business: Wealth, Ecology and the Evolutionary Corporation

Brian Nattrass and Mary Altomare (New Society Pub., 1999)
Overview of the Natural Step framework for corporate sustainability
("sustainability" is an important buzzword in many areas of non-profit and
public policy these days, as progressive organizations strive to replace short-
term planning with modes of operation that will lead to a healthier future).
Note: The Natural Step US, a non-profit dedicated to building a sustainable
future, is located in San Francisco.

Vision 2010: Forging Tomorrow's Public-Private Partnerships

The Economist Intelligence Unit (Economist Intelligence Unit, 1999)
Looks at the increasing interrelationship between government and the private
sector, as government seeks ways to lower costs and improve service.

Outsourcing State and Local Government Services

John A. O'Looney (Quorum Books, 1998)
Practical guide to outsourcing government services at the state and local level,
including advice on what to outsource and when, and how to proceed. Good
overview of the thinking behind the government-outsourcing trend.

Washington

Meg Greenfield (PublicAffairs, 2001)
Written by a Pulitzer-winning editorialist for the *Washington Post*, this is an
insightful look at the people and institutions of the District of Columbia;
worth a look for those considering moving to the Capitol.

War Stories from Capitol Hill

Colton Campbell and Paul Herrnson (Prentice Hall, 2003)
An inside look at the ins and outs of Capitol Hill by former Congressional fellows and staff.

Stories I Never Told the Speaker: The Chaotic Adventures of a Capitol Hill Aide

Marshall Lynam (Three Forks Press, 1998)
The author, who spent 36 years on Capitol Hill, recounts behind-the-scenes versions of events on the Hill.

The Complete Idiot's Guide to American Government

Mary Shaffrey and Melanie Fonder (Alpha Books, 2002)
All about the federal government and how it works. A good overview if your understanding of the different parts of government and how they interact could use some filling in on the details.

Congress for Dummies

David Silverberg, Dennis Hastert, and Tom Daschle (For Dummies, 2002)
Introduction to the players and processes of the Congress.

Power Game: How Washington Works

Hedrick Smith (Random House, 1988)
Looks at the details of how power is created and wielded in the Capitol—everything from political coalition-building to special-interest influence on politics.

Inside Congress: The Shocking Scandals, Corruption, and Abuse of Power Behind the Scenes on Capitol Hill

Ronald Kessler (Pocket Star, 1997)
Scandal! Influence peddling! Sex! All the down-and-dirtiest dirt on Washington politics.

See No Evil: The True Story of Ground Soldier in the CIA's War on Terrorism

Robert Baer (Crown Publishing Group, 2002)
Memoir of a CIA case officer with decades of experience on the ground in the Middle East.

Managing the Non-Profit Organization: Principles and Practices

Peter Drucker (HarperBusiness, 1992)
A look at the issues facing non-profit organization leaders. May be worth a look if you're considering getting into non-profit management.

Inside the CIA

Ronald Kessler (Pocket Books, 1994)
A look at the history, organization, and practices of the Central Intelligence Agency.

Not-for-Profit Accounting

Warren Ruppel (John Wiley & Sons, 2002)
A guide to non-profits' financial statements for non-accountants. May be of use in evaluating the financial health of non-profits you're considering working for.

State and Local Government: The Essentials

Richard Kearney and Ann O'm Bowman (Houghton Mifflin College, 2003)
Overview of the many issues that non-federal governments must negotiate their way through.

Storytelling for Grantseekers: The Guide to Creative Non-Profit Fundraising

Cheryl Clarke (Jossey-Bass, 2001)
If you're going into non-profit management, most likely you'll be doing fundraising. This book gives tip on how to make compelling fundraising pitches.

WetFeet®

Ten Steps to a Federal Job

Kathryn Kraemer Troutman, et al. (Resume Place Press, 2002)
Helps you evaluate your KSAs (knowledge, skills, and abilities), conform to specialized federal-jobs resume templates, and understand the hiring process at different federal agencies.

Guide to Careers in Federal Law Enforcement: Profiles of 225 High-Powered Positions and Surefire Tactics for Getting Hired

Thomas Ackerman (Hamilton Burrows Press, 2001)
Will help you figure out where you might fit in federal law enforcement and help you through often-complex hiring procedures.

Grant Writing for Dummies

Beverly Browning (For Dummies, 2001)
Thorough advice regarding grant writing, one of the cornerstones of any non-profit's operations.

Government Job Finder: Where the Jobs Are in Local, State, and Federal Government

Daniel Lauber and Jennifer Atkin (Planning Communications, 2003)
Tips on finding and applying for government jobs, at the state and local levels as well as at the federal level.

Who Will Tell the People?: The Betrayal of American Democracy

William Greider (Simon & Schuster, 1993)
Excellent, thorough (and thoroughly researched) book covering how money has taken over American politics. Definitely worth a read if you're heading to Capitol Hill, or any other area of government.

A Look over My Shoulder: A Life in the CIA

Richard Helms (Random House, 2003)

By a former director of the Agency, this book provides a look at the history of the CIA and at how the agency works.

Democracy, Bureaucracy, and the Study of Administration

Camilla Stivers (Westview Press, 2001)

Looks at the inherent tension between democracy and efficiency, and how public administration management balances that tension. Of interest to folks interested in building a career in management in government bureaucracies.

The FBI: Inside the World's Most Powerful Law Enforcement Agency

Ronald Kessler (Pocket Books, 1994)

How the FBI works, and how it evolved through its history.

The Jossey-Bass Guide to Strategic Communications for Non-Profits: A Step-by-Step Guide to Working with the Media to Generate Publicity, Enhance Fundraising, Build Membership, Change Public Policy, Handle Crises, and More!

Kathy Bonk, Henry Griggs, and Emily Tynes (Jossey-Bass, 1999)

This book will give you a leg up in conducting public relations activities for non-profits—and will give you the low-down on PR issues facing non-profit operations.

Mountains without Handrails: Reflections on the National Parks

Joseph Sax (University of Michigan Press, 1980)

History of the national parks, and overview of the tensions between the views of different segments of the population as to how the parks should be treated. Of interest to people looking at careers in the National Parks Service.

Preserving Nature in the National Parks: A History

Richard West Sellars (Yale University Press, 1999)
Should national parks serve tourists first, or the environment? A look at the tension between these two goals. Of interest to people looking at careers in the National Parks Service.

Government's Greatest Achievements: From Civil Rights to Homeland Security

Paul Charles Light (The Brookings Insitution, 2002)
Defeating polio. Rebuilding Europe after World War II. Reducing poverty among the elderly. Expanding the right to vote. Enhancing civil rights. Putting man on the moon. Despite what Rush Limbaugh might have to say about the effectiveness of government, the U.S. government has a long string of successes to be proud of. This book looks at 25 of them.

Globalization and Its Discontents

Joseph Stiglitz (W.W. Norton & Co., 2003)
This controversial book by the Nobel Prize–winning former chief economist of the World Bank looks at how the World Bank, IMF, and WTO operate—and mistakes those organizations are making, in his estimation. A must-read for anyone interested in working for those NGOs, or anyone interested in the hot-button issue of globalization.

Other Resources

Opportunity Knocks (www.opportunitynocs.org)

Leading source for non-profit jobs.

Non-Profit Career Network (www.nonprofitcareer.com)

Just as it sounds—a site with non-profit job listings, information on non-profit staffing recruiting agencies, profiles on non-profits, information on non-profit job fairs, and more.

Charity Channel's Career Search Online (http://charitychannel.com/careersearch)

Job postings.

Philanthropy Careers (http://philanthropy.com/jobs.dir/jobsmain.htm)

The jobs and career-advice site of the *Chronicle of Philanthropy*. Full of information to benefit your job search, your understanding of the non-profit arena, and so on.

Chronicle of Philanthropy (www.philanthropy.com)

One of the most popular journals for people working in the non-profit and foundation sectors—older articles can only be accessed with a subscription.

The NonProfit Times (www.nptimes.com)

News, analysis, and job listings for the non-profit sector.

The Foundation Center (www.fdncenter.org)

Information on foundations, including available grants, job opportunities, and fund-raising suggestions.

FirstGov (www.firstgov.gov)

All about working for the U.S. government, with links to federal agencies.

USA Jobs (www.usajobs.opm.gov)

The U.S. government's main job listing website. This site will help you understand how federal government hiring works, how to prepare yourself for the process through the assessment of your knowledge, skills, and abilities (KSAs) and the preparation of your federal-jobs resume, and the variety of federal job opportunities available.

Careers in Government (www.careersingovernment.com)

Another good clearinghouse for government opportunities.

govtjobs.com (www.govtjobs.com)

Information on and jobs with city, state, and county governments and other governmental jurisdictions, and access to local government executive recruiters.

LGcareers (www.lgcareers.com)

Information and advice on local government careers.

Harvard Office of Career Services Government and Politics page (www.ocs.fas.harvard.edu/resources/government)

Information and resources for people considering careers in government.

Contacting the Congress (www.visi.com/juan/congress)

A directory of members of Congress, with links to their websites, through which you can apply for internships.

Library of Congress State and Local Governments page (http://lcweb.loc.gov/global/state/stategov.html)

Links to state and local government resources and information.

U.S. Office of Personnel Management Salaries and Wages page (www.opm.gov/flsa/oca/PAYRATES/index.asp)

This page provides links to salary tables and related information for federal government jobs.

WetFeet's Insider Guide Series

Ace Your Case! The WetFeet Insider Guide to Consulting Interviews
Ace Your Case II: Fifteen More Consulting Cases
Ace Your Case III: Practice Makes Perfect
Ace Your Case IV: The Latest and Greatest
Ace Your Interview! The WetFeet Insider Guide to Interviewing
Beat the Street: The WetFeet Insider Guide to Investment Banking Interviews
Getting Your Ideal Internship
Get Your Foot in the Door! Landing the Job Interview
Job Hunting A to Z: The WetFeet Insider Guide to Landing the Job You Want
Killer Consulting Resumes!
Killer Cover Letters and Resumes!
Killer Investment Banking Resumes!
Negotiating Your Salary and Perks
Networking Works! The WetFeet Insider Guide to Networking

Career and Industry Guides

Accounting
Advertising and Public Relations
Asset Management and Retail Brokerage
Biotech and Pharmaceuticals
Brand Management
Computer Software and Hardware
Consulting for Ph.D.s, Lawyers, and Doctors
Entertainment and Sports
Health Care
Human Resources
Industries and Careers for MBAs
Industries and Careers for Undergrads
Information Technology
Investment Banking

Management Consulting
Manufacturing
Marketing and Market Research
Non-Profits and Government Agencies
Oil and Gas
Real Estate
Top 20 Biotechnology and Pharmaceutical Firms
Top 25 Consulting Firms
Top 25 Financial Services Firms
Top 20 Law Firms
Venture Capital

Company Guides

Accenture
Bain & Company
Bear Stearns
Booz Allen Hamilton
The Boston Consulting Group
Cap Gemini Ernst & Young
Citigroup
Credit Suisse First Boston
Deloitte Consulting
Goldman Sachs
IBM Business Consulting Services
JPMorgan Chase
Lehman Brothers
McKinsey & Company
Merrill Lynch
Monitor Group
Morgan Stanley